Economic Aspects of Manpower Training Programs

Theory and Policy

Daniel S. Hamermesh
Princeton University

Heath Lexington Books
D. C. Heath and Company
Lexington, Massachusetts
Toronto   London

To Frances

Table of Contents

List of Tables and Figures

Table

Figure

Preface

The hope of changing the current trends in manpower policy and research is the basic reason for writing this book. Manpower policy seems to be aimed increasingly toward providing direct help for disadvantaged workers, a purpose which, I feel, can only in the long run be wasteful, increase social conflict, and hurt the disadvantaged themselves. In the area of research the large majority of work has been performed using institutional analysis rather than the framework of standard economic analysis. I feel that economic theory has a substantial role to play in both the definition of what manpower policy should be and evaluation of existing policy. The book should provide a stimulus for additional research in this vein and for greater interest on the part of economic theorists in the problems of manpower training.

No attempt is made here to recount the vicissitudes of legislation relating to manpower training in the United States. The reader should, however, have some familiarity with past and current legislation in order to follow some of the discussion. An excellent short reference on this subject is Garth Mangum, *The Emergence of Manpower Policy* (New York: Holt, Rinehart and Winston, 1969).

In order to preserve the reader's sanity some uniformity of mathematical notation is necessary. Throughout the text parentheses ( ) denote functions, while brackets [ ] and braces { } denote that the term within brackets is to be multiplied or raised to a power.

In any endeavor of this sort there are large numbers of people who either directly or indirectly shape the author's thinking about his topic. Especially helpful to me in this respect have been Robert Goldfarb and Albert Rees, each of whom read the entire manuscript at one stage or another and offered suggestions which greatly improved the substance of the work. My colleagues, Orley Ashenfelter, Ray Fair, Frederick Harbison, Robinson Hollister, Ronald Oaxaca, and Michael Taussig, as well as Michael Borus of Michigan State University each read parts of the manuscript and provided suggestions which forced me to think through more clearly the arguments in the text. Participants in seminars at Yale University, Princeton University, the Technion of Israel, and the American Association of Agricultural Economics stimulated my thinking in several areas related to manpower training. Part of Chapter 3, appeared in the *American Economic Review* and engendered several useful comments.

This work is dependent upon both bibliographical sources and the use of computer facilities; and my research assistants and the librarians in Firestone Library provided yeoman service. Peter Maruhnic and John Wengrovius did far more than was required in helping produce the tables, and Helen Fairbanks suffered patiently through many searches for particular sources and citations. The secretaries in the Industrial Relations Section, Donna Cooper, Karen Stout, and Dorothy Silvester, performed as cryptographers in trying to decipher nearly illegible manuscripts which I gave to them.

Through a grant to the Industrial Relations Section for the study of urban labor markets the Ford Foundation financed research time and computer facilities which made the completion of this work possible.

This book is dedicated to my wife Frances, who read through the manuscript and greatly improved the clarity of the style in which it was written.

Economic Aspects of Manpower Training Programs

1 Economic Analysis and Manpower Training

The intention of this book is to use economic analysis to discuss the possible roles and effects of government intervention in the area of manpower training. These programs, which have consumed a large and expanding portion of federal appropriations in the United States, have not previously been subjected to study using the tools of modern economic analysis. We attempt in the succeeding chapters to remedy this deficiency by providing studies of manpower training as it relates to several goals of economic and social policy. Taken together, the policy conclusions which stem from our analyses suggest a redirection of manpower training policy toward goals more appropriate to such intervention in private decisions, and a more efficient use of training programs in achieving those goals.

For purposes of our discussion in this study we define manpower training programs as any government expenditures aimed directly at the labor market which increase the amount of skills embodied in workers or increase their likelihood of finding employment or a better-paying job. This definition excludes health expenditures, which surely have the property of increasing the possibility of employment, and implies the exclusion of expenditures on a formal education. Manpower programs are, then, any other allocation of resources as an investment in increasing the skills of workers, i.e., toward increasing their earnings ability either in private firms or in jobs in the public sector.

Training in the Public and the Private Sectors

Federal programs have had a long history of providing training to the private sector, but until recently training was not their acknowledged purpose. Although a number of the WPA projects of the 1930s could be classified as manpower training, they were not proposed for that purpose. Rather, their aim was mainly that of providing employment to ameliorate the effects of the Depression of the 1930s.[1] Similarly, the large-scale training of civilians for skilled work in the armed services during World War II may have increased the subsequent earning ability of many workers, but this too was not done for the purpose of training men for jobs in the private sector.

1

Only in 1961 did Congress officially acknowledge manpower training as an instrument of social and economic policy. The Area Redevelopment Act of 1961, in addition to its other features, provided subsidies for the retraining of workers who were unemployed in areas of substantial unemployment.[2] The commitment to manpower training was broadened greatly by the passage in 1962 of the Manpower Development and Training Act.[3] In this legislation Congress extended training subsidies not merely to depressed areas, but to any firm wishing to participate in the program of increasing the skills embodied in members of the labor force. This program has been supplemented and extended by the JOBS (Job Opportunities in the Business Sector) program which has expanded quite rapidly.

The Economic Opportunity Act of 1964 was designed " to mobilize the human and financial resources of the Nation to combat poverty." [4] Programs oriented toward the training of disadvantaged workers were one means of achieving this aim. The Job Corps was explicitly designed to increase the skills of disadvantaged youth; the Neighborhood Youth Corps, while directed more toward increasing employment of younger workers living in central cities, had as one of its by-products and uses the on-the-job training of these youths. The War on Poverty thus was a partial war on the insufficient skills of poorer members of society.

The magnitude of the federal commitment to manpower training is shown by the sharp increase in the size of federal appropriations for this purpose, from the inception of the MDTA in 1962 until the present time (see Table 1–1). The total size of federal participation is surely understated, for the data in our table do not include the training content of employment in the armed services.

Table 1–1. Federal Expenditures on Manpower Training Programs
(Thousands)

	Fiscal Year		
	1963[a]	1966	1969
Total	$56,070	$628,407	$1,015,939
MDTA	56,070	339,649	258,825
Institutional	55,219	281,710	196,629
OJT	851	57,939	56,429
Neighborhood Youth Corps	—	263,337	320,696
JOBS	—	—	160,821
Other	—	25,431	275,597

[a] Excludes Area Redevelopment
Source: *Manpower Report of the President*, 1970, p. 304

It is impossible to estimate the resource costs of such training in the military, for one cannot separate out from individual salaries that portion which is invested in skill development.

The size of the federal programs in itself suggests the importance of inquiring into their purposes. Although increasing the skills of workers is useful and has some economic payoff, we need to analyze the basic purposes for which this investment is being undertaken. Having determined what those goals are, we should then inquire whether existing programs have succeeded in achieving them most efficiently. An economic analysis of these two aspects, the goals of training and the efficiency of training programs, forms the substance of this book.

Federal participation in manpower training has entailed the expenditure of several billions of dollars. This figure is, however, only a small fraction of the United States' GNP. Most training takes place in the private sector in the form of on-the-job learning. When this additional part of manpower training is considered, it becomes clear that the training industry is one of the largest endeavors in a developed economy. One estimate of the gross flow of investment in on-the-job training is that in 1969 approximately $28 billion worth of resources were devoted to private training.[5] Another estimate implies that the *stock* of human capital in the form of on-the-job training embodied in the working population alone totalled nearly $150 billion in 1967.[6] Both of these estimates are probably substantial understatements, yet they illustrate the importance of training and the need for considering its effects on the economy.

Approaches to the Study of Manpower Training

What should be the role of economists and economic analysis in a discussion of social and economic policy? Three alternative approaches can be taken in the study of government-financed manpower training. Approach I consists of analyses of the legislative history of public programs and the success or failure of these programs in achieving the goals toward which they are aimed. This approach also entails the discussion of the administrative organization of public programs.[7] While both of these are important and both have occupied much of the energy of economists interested in manpower training, neither endeavor uses the core of economic analysis. Modern economics can be considered to be a set of analytical tools to be used in discussing the allocational and macroeconomic aspects of an economy. While legislative history and administrative problems can be discussed using some of these tools, economic techniques are best used in discussing government programs by analyzing the effects of these programs on individual workers, consumers, and firms.

Approach II is the analysis of the success of individual programs for manpower training. This cost-benefit analysis, if performed carefully, provides a useful service in program administration and evaluation.[8] While there are many problems of unmeasurable quantities on both the cost and benefit sides of any such analysis, this approach is superior to evaluating programs on the basis of casual observation alone.

Previous work in the area of manpower training has been confined almost exclusively to approaches I and II. The federal government funds a substantial amount of research in the area of program analysis, and the large majority of research projects supported under the provisions of the MDTA fall in this category.[9] Some of these are cost-benefit analyses which weigh both direct and indirect benefits and compare these to costs. These studies are explicitly empirical; most analyze some aspects of manpower training programs within a local area to determine whether training provides benefits exceeding the cost of the program. They consider only the primary direct and indirect effects of the program and ignore possible spillovers of the program on individuals not involved directly in it.

Another strand of empirical analysis also classifiable under approach II of our research typology uses cases to demonstrate the effects of particular programs. The usual goal of this research is to capture some of the intangible effects of manpower training through interview analysis with trainees.[10] These studies are useful in filling a gap which cannot be covered by empirical cost-benefit studies.

Both cost-benefit studies and case studies are post hoc, positive, and empirical. Their concern is with specific programs already undertaken by the federal government; they do not consider possible changes in the direction of the entire governmental effort in manpower training; nor do they apply any of the theoretical insights developed in the literature on education and training in the field of labor economics.

The third possible approach (III) for economic analysis involves not the positive evaluation of program history or effectiveness, but rather normative considerations of what constitutes appropriate and efficient government intervention in private decision making about the allocation of resources. Analyses of this sort would be much broader than simple cost-benefit analysis and would not be restricted to any individual program. Instead, they would consider the possible repercussions of intervention in specific areas in the private sector. For example, in the area of health service one might ask, "What would be the effects of a national health insurance program on the structure of the delivery of medical care?" Without discussing any particular program, such analysis would consider the effects of this program on the nation's health, on the quality of its labor force, and on other socioeconomic factors.

There are many purely economic aspects of manpower training, in both the areas where government has intervened and where training has remained in the private sector alone; and many of these are amenable to study by the methods of approach III. Training expenditures are part of the firm's labor costs. Whether the government trains in institutions or offers contracts to firms for on-the-job training, it lowers the costs of labor to the individual firm. This subsidy may induce increases in employment in the short run under certain assumptions about demand for the firm's final product. In the long run, it may also affect the amount of training offered by firms.

The skills in which the government provides training will affect the structure of employment in the private sector. For example, if the bulk of government training subsidies are provided for jobs requiring only simple skills, firms will have an incentive to substitute these jobs for those requiring more complex skills. If this incentive elicits a large response, the resulting substitution will have important effects on the structure of wages within a plant as well as on industrial relations in an individual workplace.

Differences by skill category in the amount of training subsidized will also affect the size distribution of income. If most training is concentrated in lower-level skills, incomes of already employed low-skilled workers will be driven down. Such training will, therefore, increase the skewness of the distribution of wage rates. This change will in turn affect individual decisions about desired amounts of education, so that manpower training will have an important indirect effect on the amount of formal education undertaken and thus on the need for resources in this sector.

Government subsidies for training are not distributed randomly across firms, industries, and geographical areas. For example, under a set of reimbursements for on-the-job training offered specifically for nonwhite workers, we should expect firms which discriminate less to be more involved in the training program. This greater involvement would arise because such firms would require less of an inducement to abandon their discriminatory policies in hiring. If training is given in skills more appropriate to industries which are highly labor-intensive, we would expect it to have an important effect on the capital–output ratio in the economy and therefore on the aggregate income of the economy in the future. When manpower training is concentrated in certain areas, the relative attractiveness of all areas for the location of new industry will change; and the resulting changes in the pattern of industrial location will have important secondary effects in the economy, e.g., on the transportation system.

Manpower training by the government as well as by the private sector also affects the macroeconomic performance of the economy. The role of training in removing bottlenecks in the labor market has been recognized by a number of analysts. This effect makes it clear that manpower training can have important indirect effects on the proper mix of monetary and fiscal policies as well as on a country's position in international markets.

There has been little type III research on the effects of federal programs on any of these economic aspects of manpower training. What work has been done along these lines has been of a general rather than detailed analytic nature. The foregoing considerations suggest that theoretical analysis has an important role to play in the discussion of government intervention in manpower training.

Training Goals and Analysis

Although a number of alternative goals for manpower training policy have been discussed in the literature, there has been no declaration by manpower officials or by Congress of priorities among them. Several general goals for government training programs have been cited.[11] Improving the functioning of labor-market institutions in order to increase geographical and occupational mobility is one of these. Increasing the rate of human capital formation through increased training in order to raise per capita national income is another. Many others could be offered to provide some general justification for government intervention in the private training sector.

In addition to these general goals, Congress and manpower experts have mentioned some specific purposes for training programs. Four of these will be considered here.

1. *Increasing the stock of training embodied in disadvantaged workers* to enable them to compete with other members of the labor force: Government subsidies for training these individuals can be justified on equity grounds as a means of eliminating past and current labor-market discrimination against them.

2. *Removing the excessive unemployment which pervades depressed areas*: Retraining in depressed areas is also justifiable on equity grounds, for in many areas the unemployed are victims of society's changed tastes for some local product or of the depletion of a local resource.

3. *Improving the functioning of the aggregate labor market* in order to improve macroeconomic performance: While labor supply does in the long run adjust to meet changes in demand for different skills, wage and price inflation may have such high political and possibly economic costs that

government training to improve the matching of supply and demand may be necessary.

4. *Improving the economic conditions and functioning of local labor markets in the urban areas*: Labor-force participation and mobility are dependent on the transportation network and spatial relationships of employment and residence in an urban area. The outcomes of government intervention aimed at one of these will necessarily both affect and be affected by subsidies for training.

While these four purposes are the only ones we discuss in detail, our neglect of other specific goals in no way implies that they are not amenable to analysis under the methods of approach III. As an example, fostering more rapid economic growth by increasing investment in training could be considered in detail. Also, since training diverts resources away from current consumption, problems similar to those which arise in discussing optimal *physical* capital accumulation over time could be analyzed in discussing *human* capital in general and training in particular.[12]

In each chapter, we consider the extent to which one of the above four goals has been accepted in the United States and thus the extent of its importance in shaping existing manpower programs. It is by no means clear that the public, as represented in Congress, has the same view of each goal as do professional economists. We shall therefore distinguish between these two groups in our discussion of specific goals. In addition, we shall consider the depth of commitment of Congress to each specific goal.

Although our prime interest is in manpower training, there may be other programs which could be more efficient in achieving the goals we have discussed. For example, investment and business relocation subsidies could be more useful in reducing unemployment in depressed areas than the retraining of unemployed workers. We shall, therefore, compare manpower training with alternative means of achieving these goals.

To present detailed economic studies of all aspects of each goal would require many volumes. For example, training programs designed to help disadvantaged workers have a number of economic effects, each of which could be considered in a theoretical study. Subsidies for disadvantaged workers affect the employment prospects of other, " nonsubsidized " workers; they also affect the income distribution in society. For each of these effects one could construct a model with normative implications about the directions manpower training should take to achieve the goal of helping disadvantaged workers without hurting the rest of society. Rather than discussing every economic aspect of each goal in detail, we shall present a detailed analysis of one or several narrower aspects of each of the four specific goals.

Because there is a lack of data on the effects of training on the supply of labor for specific jobs, and because it is impossible to measure the costs of training, most of our analysis uses pure theory and simulation studies rather than direct empirical work. Each of the four studies is designed either to show possible efficient ways of achieving each goal or to illustrate a particular economic problem that might arise out of attempts to use manpower training to attain the goal in question.

Although most of the discussion relates specifically to training in the United States, the analytical parts of each chapter are of complete generality. For example, our discussion of the appropriate skills to be subsidized by government training programs in order to remove labor-market bottlenecks could be applied to any developed country. Similarly, a consideration of the effects of subsidized training for disadvantaged workers, though applied in the context of helping nonwhites, could be applied equally well to subsidization aimed at any population group against which economic discrimination has been practiced.

In Chapter 2, we discuss the displacement of "nonsubsidized" workers by "subsidized" workers. If there is no excess demand for a firm's product, some amount of displacement will occur whenever a training subsidy is granted. The displacement problem imparts unknowable biases to any cost-benefit study. Since it is impossible to hold constant changing demand and other variable factors, one cannot adequately measure the extent of the displacement in any empirical work. One can, however, build a simple model of a firm's employment, wage, and training decisions and use this model to simulate the conditions under which a subsidy for training disadvantaged workers would lead to more or less displacement. This knowledge should prove of value in minimizing the political dangers inherent in the displacement phenomenon.

The analysis in Chapter 3 considers conditions in a depressed area under which a market-wide wage subsidy, one paid throughout a worker's tenure in the firm, would create more employment than would a market-wide training subsidy, one paid at the time at which the worker is hired. The relative merits of these alternative subsidies are analyzed under fairly general assumptions about the nature of training in the subsidized firms in both the short and long runs.

The main purpose of Chapter 4 is to construct a multisector macro-economic model of wages and employment. Government training subsidies affect the time paths of these endogenous variables through the elasticities of labor supply to the sectors which make up the model. In the simulations, we examine the most efficient way of spending a fixed sum of money on training labor. The decision criterion is that of maximizing a shift in the short-run trade-off between inflation and unemployment over the entire range of unemployment. The various parameters of this simulated model represent the cyclical nature of product demand, the labor intensity of the sector, the supply elasticities of labor to each sector, and the lags in adjustment of employment to output. For each of these we analyze the conditions under which the maximum shift in the trade-off can be obtained. Our results thus provide the first real evidence about this important objective of manpower training subsidies.

In Chapter 5, we discuss the role of manpower training programs as they apply particularly to an urban area. We attempt to isolate those aspects of manpower training which are quite divorced from the demographic character of an urban area and affect instead its spatial aspects. Perhaps most important is the fact that labor markets are to some extent self-contained units which should, if the economy is to function efficiently, also be working in a fairly efficient way. For that reason we analyze what characteristics influence patterns of voluntary mobility within a metropolitan area and discover which areas have unusually high or low mobility. This information should be useful in pinpointing cities where manpower training programs should be concentrated. The relation between training and transportation in determining the labor supply in an area is also discussed.

Although each of the specific goals could be important for manpower training, there has been no consideration of which goals might be most suitably attacked by training programs. Chapter 6 presents an analysis of possible conflicts among the goals and discusses whether all of them can be achieved simultaneously. Those goals which are most appropriately met by manpower training are then discussed in greater detail, and a number of specific changes in existing manpower programs as well as indications for future programs are suggested.

As is clear from this discussion, each chapter contains both a general consideration of the goal in question as well as a specific analytical study of some economic aspect of that goal. Because of this dual approach there are a number of sections of the study which can be skipped by the reader who is not interested in the details of economic analysis (specifically, pages 27–37, 46–58, 68–82, and 97–105). The remaining parts of each chapter contain less technical economic discussions of training and considerations of training policy.

2 Jobs for Disadvantaged Workers and the Displacement Problem

The goal of increasing employment among disadvantaged groups has often been cited as a primary purpose of manpower policy. Despite the importance of government attempts to achieve this goal, it is nonetheless necessary to analyze the secondary effects of policies in this direction, for they may be important both for program evaluation and for political reasons. We shall, therefore, discuss conditions when subsidies for training these workers produce a greater or lesser displacement of "nonsubsidized" workers.

The most useful way to proceed with such an analysis would involve the construction of a regression model. Unfortunately, however, sufficient information simply does not exist. Instead of constructing this model we can build a simplified theoretical structure which, we hope, captures the major elements of the displacement problem. Using this model we can then simulate the conditions under which subsidies to employ disadvantaged workers will cause displacement of workers for whom the firms do not receive a subsidy.

The simulation model which we construct is rather abstract, but it does have some important implications for policy in the area of manpower training. Assuming that increased employment among disadvantaged groups is desirable, the government should try to tailor its programs to achieve this goal most efficiently. Our model provides some insights into the types of firms in which training subsidies will produce the greatest increase in employment among lower income groups. If the loci of government training subsidies are not determined in a purely political fashion, this information should enable a manpower program to achieve greater efficiency in the training of disadvantaged workers.

Program Goals and Their Attainment

The analysis in this chapter can be applied to any manpower subsidy program which increases the employability of disadvantaged workers. Subsidized on-the-job training under the MDTA and the JOBS programs certainly comes under this rubric, for in these programs firms are given an incentive to train workers who qualify for the subsidy. Institutional programs in the MDTA also qualify, for in them the placement activities of the program lower the

11

search costs to employers and thus increase the likelihood of disadvantaged workers being hired in place of "nonsubsidized" workers. The Jobs Corps increases the likelihood of subsidy-trained workers being employed in place of "nonsubsidized" workers, and as such can also be analyzed in terms of the model constructed here. Even programs aimed primarily at job creation, such as the Neighborhood Youth Corps, may be included in this analysis, for they too increase the probability that disadvantaged enrollees will find useful employment in the private sector at a later time.

The goal of increasing employment among disadvantaged groups has become more important as the manpower programs of the federal government have expanded. Indeed, its importance was recognized in the proposed revisions of the Manpower Act in 1965 introduced by Senator Clark: "The manpower, employment, and training problems of worker groups such as the long-term unemployed, disadvantaged youth, displaced older workers, the handicapped, members of minority groups, and other similar groups," [1] all were recognized as being of importance for manpower policy.

The special importance of training disadvantaged youth has also been recognized. Presumably the rationale for this special recognition is the hope that training these workers while they are young will have significant generational effects on the problem of poverty. Aside from this economic goal, it was recognized quite early that untrained, unemployed youth posed special problems for society: "I do not need to point out...that if we do not train them, the alternatives are that they will be on the street corners, they will move then into juvenile delinquency of one kind or another, and they will turn into prospects that are so serious that we have got to do something about it." [2]

For each group which might be classified as disadvantaged, the percentage of training funds allocated to the group has increased over the lifetime of the federal training programs. This increase is apparent in Table 2–1, which shows the percent distributions by various categories of manpower expenditures in selected years. The percentage of the very young among enrollees in MDTA institutional programs increased from 6 percent in 1963 to over 12 percent in 1969. A similar increase was observable in on-the-job training among youth. There was a rise from somewhat over 8 percent to 11 percent in on-the-job training slots allocated to workers aged 18 or less.

In the case of the racial distribution of trainees, there has been a substantial rise in the proportion of federal funds used for training nonwhite members of the labor force. Nonwhites constituted nearly half of the institutional trainees in 1969, while they were slightly less than a quarter of those trainees in 1963. Although the percentages are lower in the case of OJT, there was also a doubling in the percent of the total trained who were nonwhite.

Table 2–1. Characteristics of Trainees Enrolled in Institutional and On-the-Job Programs Under the MDTA
(Percent distributions)

| | Fiscal Year of Enrollment | | | | | |
| | 1963 | | 1966 | | 1969 | |
	Institutional	OJT	Institutional	OJT	Institutional	OJT
Age:						
Under 19	6.3	8.2	15.9	16.5	12.5	11.1
19–21	19.1	22.9	22.2	23.1	25.0	25.0
22–34	43.9	44.1	35.3	38.1	38.2	40.6
35 and older	30.7	24.8	26.6	22.3	24.3	23.3
Race:						
White	76.5	83.0	62.5	76.2	55.9	61.1
Nonwhite	23.5	17.0	37.5	23.8	44.1	38.9
Years of Schooling:						
Under 8	3.1	6.4	6.7	6.2	9.0	7.5
8	7.6	9.2	9.6	8.0	9.8	9.0
9–11	30.0	28.7	35.7	28.7	38.8	35.0
12 and over	59.3	55.7	48.0	57.1	42.4	48.5

Source: Based on *Manpower Report of the President,* 1970, pp. 308, 310.

Table 2–1 also shows that the patterns of change in the distribution of trainees by educational attainment are significantly different for the institutional and OJT programs. Between 1963 and 1969, the percentage of institutional trainees who had less than 8 years of education tripled, from 3 percent to 9 percent. In the case of OJT, however, the percentage of such trainees remained more or less constant.

The importance of the disadvantaged in current manpower programs is underscored by the data in Table 2–2 concerning the Neighborhood Youth Corps out-of-school program and the JOBS contractual program. In both of these programs, the percentage of nonwhites is vastly greater than the nonwhite representation in the labor force. Moreover, in the increasingly important JOBS program the overwhelming majority of trainees are nonwhite. In addition, the bulk of enrollees in this program are below average in age and have at most a high-school education.

It appears that there has been a general increase in the proportion of trainees who might be classified as disadvantaged. One might argue that while this increase does reflect a conscious decision by government, it is an indirect

**Table 2–2. Characteristics of Trainees Enrolled in Neigh-
borhood Youth Corps (Out-of-School) and JOBS (Contracts) Programs**
(Percent distributions)

| | Fiscal Year of Enrollment | | | |
| | 1969 | | 1970 | |
	NYC	JOBS	NYC	JOBS
Age:				
Under 19	63	17	91	17
19–21	34	31	7	30
22–44	3	48	2	48
45 and older	—	4	—	5
Race:				
White	48	13	50	18
Nonwhite	52	87	50	82
Years of Schooling:				
Under 9	27	14	32	15
9–11	69	54	66	51
12 and over	4	32	2	34

Source: Manpower Administration, Office of Manpower Management Data Systems, unpublished data reported in Bureau of
National Affairs, *Manpower Information Service*, January 13, 1971.

result of the decreased unemployment in the economy over the period which
we observed. The apparent increase in the government's interest in training
disadvantaged groups might merely be caused by the possibility that these
groups are the only ones who could not find jobs at the relatively low unemployment rate prevailing in 1969. It is, of course, impossible to refute that
claim on the basis of this table alone. Nonetheless, the emphasis in the statements quoted above indicates that this goal has affected government policy to
a great extent.

It is important that training programs designed to employ disadvantaged
workers do not merely shuffle jobs now held by other low-skilled workers to
the presently unemployed disadvantaged workers or place disadvantaged
workers instead of better-off unemployed workers who would be hired in
the absence of a subsidy. This redistribution of jobs might occur if there were
a surplus of more-qualified workers in the occupations for which the subsidy
programs are training disadvantaged workers. If such a reshuffling took

place, one might well imagine that congressional resistance to further appropriations for these training programs would be increased. This decline in
appropriations would decrease the possibility of attaining the goal of
providing jobs for the disadvantaged.

As early as 1962, when the MDTA was being debated, a number of congressmen voiced concern over the possibility of reshuffling. One stated,
"Other interesting occupations here are dishwashers, cleaning occupations,
policemen, kitchen workers, laundry workers, cheesemakers, and etc. I
understand that we have quite a surplus of cheese now but we are going to be
training more cheesemakers." [3] Another legislator feared that these training
subsidies would simply take the place of existing, privately run OJT programs.
He felt, "the banks will continue to train their tellers, the railroads and
airlines their ticket agents, and the grocery stores their clerks. These and a
host of others of a similar nature are on this list [of occupations certified as
having an excess demand] as made available by the Labor Department." [4]
These sentiments make it clear that the feedback from displaced employees to
their congressmen could have important detrimental effects on the future of
the training efforts. There might be decreased appropriations for training or,
another possibility, a turning away of the training programs from the goal of
helping to increase employment among disadvantaged workers. This feedback
effect is thus very important, and it provides the justification for analyzing
displacement in greater detail.

In the general case, one might imagine the feedback effect working in the
following manner: (1) A program, either instituted by the executive branch
or enacted by Congress, aids one particular segment of the population.
(2) This program has some detrimental effects on other segments of the
population, and these become apparent at some point after the program is
instituted. (3) These groups which feel hurt by the program are powerful
enough to bring pressure that causes either an end to the program or substantial modifications in it.

There are a number of examples in which the feedback effect has been
apparent. The mineral depletion allowance is one outstanding case. This
allowance aids firms engaged in mineral exploration but has the detrimental
effect of raising the tax bills of other industries and of private individuals.
Although it took many years to achieve success, opposition to the allowance
became powerful enough in 1969 to cause a substantial reduction in the
percentage which the firms could write off their tax bills. [5] The Department of
the Interior issued leases to oil companies to permit the drilling of wells in
offshore areas. While this program certainly aided the oil companies, its
detrimental effects on private citizens became painfully apparently in the rash
of oil spills that took place shortly after drilling began. This effect led to a

suspension of drilling and to the resumption of drilling under much more stringent safety requirements.[6] The quotas on oil imports imposed in the late 1950s have generated increasing opposition by consumers hurt by higher fuel prices, and it appears that this may result in their suspension in the 1970s.

In conclusion, unless the displacement of "nonsubsidized" workers by subsidy-trained disadvantaged individuals is minimized, our examples would indicate that the goal of employing the disadvantaged might either be abandoned or modified. As has often been pointed out, the existence of unemployed workers congregated in urban areas does not help to further the achievement of a more stable society. For this reason, any policy which can increase the employment of these workers (and minimization of the displacement of "nonsubsidized" members of the labor force is clearly one such policy) will be of use in easing social conflict.

Displacement in a Labor Market

In discussing displacement we shall compare dynamic equilibria in a firm. We shall look at the firm's employment of both "subsidized" workers (those originally employed under a government training subsidy) and "nonsubsidized" workers (those employed without subsidy) after the subsidy has been offered and after all adjustments have taken place. This level of employment can then be compared to the level of employment prevailing before the subsidy was applied. Throughout we will assume that we have abstracted from technical change and other shifts in factor demand that might affect employment.

We define displacement to be a decline in employment of nonsubsidized workers relative to the number of disadvantaged workers who receive employment under the subsidy program. For example, a certain set of training allowances may lead one firm to employ 100 workers who qualify for the training allowance during their initial employment. If the employment of these 100 workers eventually leads to an increase of only 25 in the firm's total employment, then we know that 75 nonsubsidized workers have been displaced. We thus say that there has been a 75 percent displacement effect of this particular training program.

A distinction must be made between direct and indirect displacement. We define direct displacement as the substitution of disadvantaged workers for currently employed workers. This substitution is highly unlikely, for a rational firm will only make this change if the subsidy is large enough to cover *both* the general and the specific training of the disadvantaged workers. Only if both of these costs are covered will it pay the firm to scuttle its fixed investment in specific training embodied in its current employees. Indirect displacement occurs when a subsidized firm hires untrained, disadvantaged workers in preference to more skilled unemployed who do not qualify for employment under a training subsidy.

There are three separate determinants of the displacement that might be produced by a subsidy to one particular group of workers. The first is the direct effect on the firm's choice of inputs. Assuming a constant rate of output, the subsidy acts to lower the relative price of labor and thus decrease the capital–labor ratio in the firm. If the increase in total employment is enough to offset the number of disadvantaged workers employed, there is no displacement effect at all. If, however, this is not the case, there will be displacement of nonsubsidized workers.

If the subsidy is not scattered randomly among all firms in the economy but rather is concentrated among certain firms, there is also the possibility that employment will increase as a whole even though output does not change. If the subsidy is given mainly to firms employing a relatively labor-intensive technology, these firms will expand their output at the expense of firms employing a relatively capital-intensive technology. If this occurs, employment in the economy will increase while its physical capital-labor ratio will decrease. This "composition-of-output" effect might be sufficient to prevent displacement when a subsidy program is instituted.

The third determinant might be called the aggregate-demand effect. It is possible that a subsidized training program will increase the government's demand for goods and services and also increase the economy-wide marginal propensity to consume; thus, aggregate demand will increase because of the training program. This increase would lead to increased real output if the economy were at less than full employment and would thus lead to increased employment as well. Even in this case, however, it is by no means clear that this upward shift in aggregate demand would produce an increase in employment sufficient to prevent displacement of nonsubsidized workers.

In the analysis that follows we shall not consider the possibility that aggregate demand increases as a result of the subsidy to firms to train disadvantaged workers. On the one hand, there is no evidence that the marginal propensity to consume is greater for lower income groups.[7] There is thus no reason for the increase in employment among these groups to lead to an increase in the aggregate marginal propensity to consume as the proportion of income received by such groups increases. Furthermore, the training program would probably have only a slight effect on government purchases of goods and services. The major component of government training subsidies is a transfer payment from taxpayers to firms and to the workers receiving training allowances. Indeed, some observers have pointed out, "that it is difficult to place much faith in the power of employment expansion effects of retraining without increasing aggregate demand."[8] Without any additional programs designed to increase government spending it is doubtful that training programs alone can achieve much in this direction for any more than short periods of time. For this reason, we shall ignore this possible effect throughout the remainder of our discussion.

We also do not consider the possibility that training of disadvantaged workers is in occupations which are in shortage, although this may be true. (Evidence against this proposition is, however, presented in Chapters 4 and 6, and a full-blown model with this assumption relaxed is constructed in Chapter 4.) Rather, we assume here that the subsidy does not help to remove skill bottlenecks and thus does not help to increase employment through the mechanism of matching new trainees with *truly* vacant jobs. All of our conclusions in this chapter rest on the assumption that training is given in jobs in which there is no real shortage of labor.

Even if there were some positive short-run aggregate demand effect of the training subsidy, displacement in the short run would still be a problem. While there would be no loss of employment among nonsubsidized workers, there would be a shift of employment of this group away from firms receiving the subsidy and toward firms which do not participate in the training program. There would thus be some short-run displacement of workers, and this effect might be sufficient to generate enough dissatisfaction with the training program to cause its curtailment.

We shall return later to the discussion of the composition-of-output effect. Clearly, if the government can concentrate its training in labor-intensive areas, such a policy will, other things equal, be beneficial. The effects of such a concentration are thus important for a consideration of the magnitude of the displacement produced by a training subsidy.

The main concern of our model will be with the effects of a training subsidy on the employment of different factors of production by a firm producing a constant output. The analysis will be confined to the micro-economic level and will examine how a decrease in the price of disadvantaged labor affects the employment of nonsubsidized labor and capital, as well as how it affects the wage paid by the firm and the amount of training the firm offers. We do not examine the effects of the program on incomes of the trainees, nonsubsidized workers, and displaced workers. This examination would be much more difficult than the analysis of employment alone and is no more interesting in its implications for the political effects of training programs.

The Effects of Displacement on Program Evaluation

Previous work in the area of the analysis of manpower training has been confined chiefly to cost-benefit studies of particular programs and of programs on a national scale. (These studies form the bulk of the Type II training research discussed in Chapter 1.) In all of these studies, the displacement problem is important for judging the results of the analysis, and all of the analysts recognize the possible biases in their results which might be caused by displacement of nonsubsidized workers. Two alternative approaches have been taken with regard to the role of displacement in the evaluation of training programs. On the one hand, several analysts have assumed that displacement was either nonexistent or of only minor importance and have concluded that the results of the cost-benefit analysis have not been biased by displacement. Others have admitted that the magnitude of the effect of displacement on the results cannot be known and have gone ahead to present the results with the caveat that they may be very strongly biased.

Particularly prominent among the first category of treatment of displacement were a number of early (pre–1966) studies of specific programs under the MDTA and the Area Redevelopment Act. For example, Page treated the displacement problem by assuming, "in the analysis that there would be no displacement of workers as a result of retraining."[9] Borus assumed that the effects of displacement on his results were unimportant. He argued that the occupations in which training takes place are those certified by the State Employment Service as being fields in which there is an excess demand for labor. Since during the period which he observed there were no changes in the list of shortage occupations certified by the State Employment Service, he concluded that these occupations were ones in which the governmentally subsidized trainees would find jobs without displacing existing workers.[10] Given the difficulties inherent in defining shortages, the failure of most firms to participate in State Employment Service programs and the very loose labor market which prevailed after the training period, this conclusion must be taken lightly.

In the most comprehensive discussion to date of manpower policy in the United States, Levitan and Mangum state, "Lacking evidence, it is reasonable to assume that some substitution may have occurred in the slack labor markets of 1963–64, but not to a significant extent in the tighter ones of 1966–67, with 1965 as a period of transition between the two situations."[11] Certainly, it is valid to assume that there were many more occupations during the latter period in which excess demand existed, and for this reason one cannot disagree with the statement that displacement was less in the latter period. Nonetheless, displacement may have been important even in this time of quite low unemployment if the particular occupations for which training was being offered were not those in which shortages existed. The difficulties of defining a shortage and the lack of evidence that the occupations in which training was being offered were those where "shortages" existed lead one to assume that even the second period could well have been characterized by significant displacement effects.

Cain and Stromsdorfer are typical of those who admit the impossibility of finding out the magnitude of the displacement effect. Unfortunately, their analysis is confused by the statement, "that a final justification for the assumption that the unemployment experiences of the non-trainees are not affected by what happened to the trainees is simply that the number of trainees is small, a few thousand, compared to the tens of thousands of males and females of these age and skill groups."[12] A small program to train unemployed workers will have only a small absolute effect on the job opportunities of currently employed workers. Its relative effects, however, could very well be just as large as those of a larger program. Unless a shortage is small enough to be removed entirely by a training program, there is no reason to assume that the magnitude of a program affects the percentage displacement to which it gives rise.

Taking a pessimistic view, Goldfarb discusses the conditions under which displacement could be measured.[13] He maintains that the only way to analyze the effects of a subsidy program on the nonsubsidized workers in an area is to compare employment experiences in that area to an identical area in which the subsidy is not being offered. Since it is, of course, impossible to create two identical areas, one receiving the subsidy and the other not, his view is thus one of very serious doubt as to the possibility of measuring the displacement effect.

Although existing data and training programs do not permit this measurement, there is no need for a negative view about the possibility of ever being able to measure displacement empirically. One might, for example, conduct an experiment which would allow collection of enough data to measure the displacement caused by a specific subsidy. The government might train some fixed number of jobless individuals in one city and none in another, widely separated city. For each of the cities detailed data might be collected on migration (to account for workers attracted by the prospect of employment induced by the subsidy), on the employment experience of each individual in each town, on the national increase in demand for products of the type made in each town and on the incomes received by each individual in each town. In short, one might be able to collect enough data to estimate supply and demand curves for different types of labor in the two labor markets. One might then compare how these curves have been shifted in the one market by the introduction of the subsidy for training unemployed workers.

Such an experimental approach is not unreasonable nor unprecedented. The well-known negative income tax experiment is surely no more expensive than that required to estimate the displacement effect of training subsidies.[14] Within the area of training itself the government has already proposed an experiment designed to estimate the effects of alternative methods of providing payments to firms for training disadvantaged workers.[15] Both of these experiments are probably no less costly than one that would be needed to measure displacement; the real problem with measuring displacement is correctly specifying what data would have to be collected during the course of the experiment.

Formulation of the Model

We assume that there are three factors of production: (1) Homogeneous capital, (2) labor which is homogeneous after it has been hired and trained by the firm, and (3) specific training. This last includes both the training costs for Becker-type specific training and the costs of search incurred by the firm when it seeks new workers.[16] The training costs thus include many expenditures borne by the firm during the initial period of a worker's employment. We also assume that these three factors are combined in a Cobb–Douglas-type production function, one in which the elasticities sum to unity. The incorporation of a unitary elasticity of substitution between capital and labor (training and raw labor together) appears to be justified by a number of empirical studies.[17] There is some evidence which tentatively suggests that the elasticity of substitution between raw labor and education is significantly greater than one.[18] If this result also held between raw labor and specific training, it would suggest that we should expand our production function to include a unitary elasticity between capital and labor, but some greater elasticity between the two components of labor in our model. The implications of this possibility for our results on the displacement effect of training subsidies are discussed below.

In this model, the firm faces a supply curve of untrained, nonsubsidized labor which is infinitely elastic at a wage rate equal to one. We are thus assuming that there is no labor shortage in the occupations in which the firm's employees fall. Clearly, if there is a shortage, if the demand curve for this occupation cuts the short-run supply curve in its vertical part, no displacement will occur. In addition to this wage rate of one which is paid to any unskilled employee the firm also pays a premium (m) to its employees to induce them not to quit. There is some optimal premium determined by the nature of the quits function and the amount of specific training costs which the firm faces. The assumption of a single, constant premium paid to all employees who have completed training is an abstraction necessary to maintain simplicity in our model. It detracts little from the usefulness of our results, however, for in equilibrium there will be an explicit, unchanging relation between the duration of employment and the wage. Our use of a single m may be viewed as summarizing a whole range of premia, just as the use of one specific training figure summarizes what is surely a function relating specific training to job tenure.

We assume that the quit rate in the firm is

$$q = q(m) \qquad q' < 0, q'' > 0 \tag{2.1}$$

where q is the turnover rate. The negative slope of this function is based on the cross-sectional evidence in the studies by Burton and Parker and by Pencavel.[19] The positive second derivative can be justified by an appeal to the worker's perception of increases in m. The Weber–Fechner theory of perception states that proportional increments to a stimulus produce decreasingly strong responses. If we view the wage premium as the stimulus and the quit rate as the response, this psychological theory suggests that the quits function should be convex. Quits will decrease at a decreasing rate as the wage paid by the firm increases above the market wage for unskilled labor. This relationship is depicted in Figure 2–1.

Perhaps the most important feature of this model is its definition of training costs and their role in affecting employment and wage rates. We assume that there are ordinary specific costs of S for each nonsubsidized worker who might be employed by the firm. These costs include the above-mentioned specific training costs, the costs of processing the new worker, and the costs of finding him. The sum of these costs is by no means trivial. As Table 2–3 shows, the estimates of the hiring-costs component alone range as high as $1,100 in one instance. This measure does not include the cost of training specific to the firm, a cost which would substantially raise the figures presented in the table.

In addition to these ordinary training costs, which must be paid for all workers hired by the firm, we can postulate that there are extra costs which the firm must incur if it hires disadvantaged employees. Clearly, if these extra costs exist and are not offset by subsidies, the infinitely elastic supply of workers in this labor-surplus occupation who do not require these extra costs ensures that disadvantaged workers will not be employed. There are a number of reasons why the specific training costs which the firm must pay if it hires disadvantaged workers are greater than those it faces for other employees.

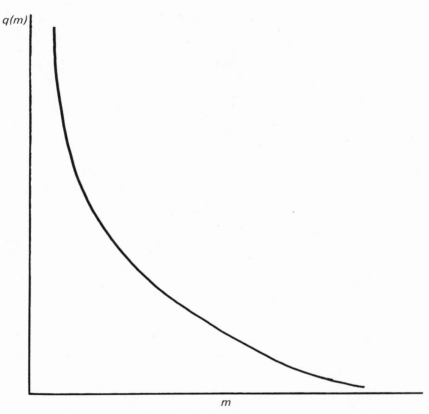

Figure 2-1. Relationship Between the Wage Premium and the Quit Rate.

Table 2–3. Average Hiring Costs by Occupation and Industry, Monroe County, New York (Rochester) 1965–1966

Occupation group	Manufacturing	Nonmanufacturing
Professional, managerial, and technical workers	$1,139	$292
Clerical workers	150	130
Skilled workers	537	103
Semiskilled and unskilled workers	92	94
All occupations	222	138

Source: John G. Myers, *Job Vacancies in the Firm and the Labor Market* (New York, National Industrial Conference Board, 1969), p. 31.

One might define "disadvantaged workers" as those who have the least general training embodied in them. Such workers are less able to complete the specific training in the firm than are ordinary workers. For this reason, any effort to give them the specific training would result in substantial extra costs in terms of lost output and additional instruction time on the part of current employees.

Disadvantaged workers are also harder for many firms to find, a fact very often cited in popular literature on the problems of urban ghettoes.[20] Therefore search costs, one major component of the variable S, are likely to be higher for disadvantaged workers. Even if there were no other economic reasons for the extra hiring costs associated with disadvantaged workers, the very fact that current employees might be prejudiced against disadvantaged

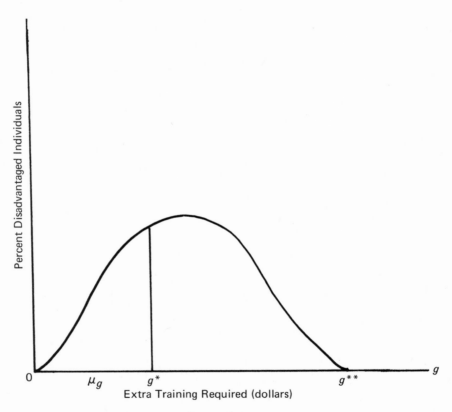

Figure 2-2. The Distribution of Disadvantaged Workers.

(often nonwhite) workers might create a situation in which these workers are not hired. The profit-maximizing firm will be inclined not to hire disadvantaged workers if doing so causes loss of employee morale and results in lower output.[21] Thus, the analysis of displacement is formally identical whether or not disadvantaged status is solely the result of current labor-market discrimination. The policy prescriptions, of course, differ drastically.

Although these costs may exist for each disadvantaged worker, it appears reasonable to assume that they vary substantially among individuals in the disadvantaged group. Some workers who might receive a subsidy would require only slightly more training and hiring expenditures than would nonsubsidized workers. On the other hand, there are those individuals for whom the extra expenditures have to be rather substantial. Without any additional knowledge about the distribution of training costs we postulate that they range in the population of disadvantaged individuals from zero extra costs up to some number g^{**}, probably a fairly high figure. We do not assume that g^{**} is infinite, as even for a completely unskilled worker who is unemployed there is undoubtedly some finite sum which characterizes the extra training costs the firm must incur if it were to hire him. Furthermore, we postulate that these extra expenditures are distributed as the probability function h

$$\int_0^{g^{**}} h(g)\,dg = 1$$

with the shape shown in Figure 2–2.

Specification of the Subsidy

Although our discussion proceeds in terms of on-the-job training, the analysis is equally applicable to the displacement effects of institutional training. By increasing the skills embodied in disadvantaged workers, institutional programs enable them to compete with and, if there are no shortages, displace nonsubsidized individuals. Moreover, in providing firms with qualified trainees the government saves employers the specific costs of search.

Actual OJT subsidies under the MDTA are administered using complicated sets of schedules defining the amount to be reimbursed to employers under the program. These schedules, coupled with the fixed appropriations set by Congress, produce some number of available training slots. The actual allocation of individual trainees among firms depends upon the availability of the trainees in the areas where the firms are located and on a comparison of the benefits the firm might receive from training to the costs thereof. These costs include both monetary costs and nonpecuniary costs, so that one might expect trainees to be allocated disproportionately to those firms in which nonpecuniary cost factors, such as racial discrimination, are less important.

In our model, we set up a stylized version of the actual reimbursement procedure. We assume that the program has targeted certain firms to receive the subsidies, that the appropriations are allocated among them in some way, and that the subsidy each firm receives is fixed in amount. We then examine whether objective characteristics of a firm, such as the parameters of its production function and its quits function, are related to the amount of displacement. Our results will be accurate reflections of the program's true effects as long as nonpecuniary factors which might affect the allocation of training money among firms are not related to the objective characteristics.

In summary, we view the government as selecting a firm and giving it some fixed amount of money to subsidize the training of disadvantaged workers. We then inquire as to how many disadvantaged workers are hired, how many nonsubsidized workers are employed, and what happens in a comparative static analysis to the capital stock in the firm, the specific training given by the firm, and the wage rate that it pays.

In this model, the average extra training costs for disadvantaged workers lie somewhere between zero and g^*, the maximum extra training required for any disadvantaged worker who qualifies under the program. (Individuals for whom $g > g^*$ will be excluded from the program.) We assume in specifying how the subsidy is to be applied that the government seeks to employ the entire group of disadvantaged workers in the firm selected to receive the subsidy. Since the government wishes to see all the workers in the group employed, it must either price discriminate by paying that g appropriate for each worker, or pay an average of g^* for each worker which it wishes to have hired. We assume that in actuality the government does not price discriminate, but rather allows firms to reap some surplus on workers whose extra training requirement is less than g^*. This assumption is quite a reasonable one for a profit-maximizing firm, and it is consistent with the observed "creaming" of the most able workers who qualify for the subsidy which apparently characterizes all of the federal on-the-job training programs.[22]

The marginal labor cost for the least able disadvantaged worker being subsidized under this program is

$$[1 + m] + q(m)[S + g^*]$$

The first term in the above expression is the wage paid to this group for each period, and the second term might be identified as the user cost of the total training and hiring expenditures on this individual. The firm will receive for this individual g^* during the period in which he is hired, a sum just enough to bring his labor costs into equality with those for nonsubsidized workers.

For an individual whose extra training costs are less than g^* the firm receives an amount g^* when the man is hired but need only pay some amount less than that in hiring and training him. On the average, the firm thus makes an extra profit per period per worker over his tenure in the firm of

$$q(m)[g^* - \mu_g]$$

where μ_g is the extra training required for the average potential trainee whose extra training is less than g^*, and the quit rate is the inverse of the average duration of employment in the firm.

As we noted above, the term $[g^* - \mu_g]$ would probably approach g^* in the absence of tight governmental control. Profit-maximizing firms will, unless they are controlled by the agency allocating the subsidy, attempt to hire those disadvantaged workers for whom the profit on training is likely to be greater. It thus seems most reasonable to assume that the training subsidy in this type of program will generate substantial profits for those firms which are involved in the program.

More important from our viewpoint is whether the quantity $[g^* - \mu_g]$ varies across firms. In particular, if it is correlated with some of the objective characteristics of the firms which we try to analyze, our results may well be biased. There is no way of knowing the extent to which this correlation exists, for the actual degree of correlation depends upon the difficulties of training disadvantaged workers in different firms.

Since we have no knowledge about how the extra training requirement varies across firms, we simulate the model for each of three separate assumptions about this correlation. Case I assumes that the extra training requirement $[g^* - \mu_g]$ is constant among all possible combinations of the parameters characterizing the firms. In Case II, the extra training varies with $\sqrt{S}$, the square root of the specific training in the firm. Case III assumes that this correlation is with the actual amount, S, of the training costs for ordinary, nonsubsidized workers. We base this relation on training costs because it seems likely that in those firms which spend a substantial amount on search and specific training the required ability of the prospective employees must be at least somewhat higher. Furthermore, this correlation between general training and specific training or hiring costs has been pointed out in the literature on training and wages.[23]

Displacement in the Short Run

Before we move ahead to analyze the more interesting case of the firm's long-run adjustment to the training subsidy, we first consider the case of the short run. We ask the question: To what extent does a subsidy for disadvantaged workers affect the employment of nonsubsidized workers for a firm in which the capital stock is constant at some K^* *and* the amount of specific training cost is constant at some S^*? The only adjustments the firm can make are in its total employment and in the wage it pays its workers.

The firm's profits in the short run are

$$\pi = f(E + E') - [1 + m][E + E'] - q(m)[E + E']S^* + q(m)[g^* - \mu_g]E' \quad (2.2)$$

where we have collapsed the production function to include only total employment as its argument and have assumed an infinitely elastic product demand at a price of one. The introduction of the particular number does not detract from the generality of the result, but our use of competition in the product market does. E is nonsubsidized and E' is subsidized employment. To discover the effects of the subsidy on total employment we analyze the profit-maximizing employment which results, first in the case in which no subsidy is received, i.e., in which E' equals zero, and then in the case in which the firm receives a subsidy to employ E' additional workers. We differentiate equation (2.2) with respect to employment in both cases to find the firm's equilibrium point. In the unsubsidized case, the equilibrium employment is

$$E_0^* = f'^{-1}(1 + m_0^* + q(m_0^*)S^*) \quad (2.3)$$

where m_0^* is the wage premium the firm chooses in this case. In the subsidized case, the firm maximizes profits by choosing some optimal number of non-subsidized employees to use in addition to the E' subsidized employees. This condition results in a total employment of

$$E_1^* + E' = f'^{-1}(1 + m_1^* + q(m_1^*)S^*) \quad (2.4)$$

where m_1^* is the wage premium chosen in the case in which the firm receives the training subsidy.

As is apparent from equations (2.3) and (2.4), the firm's employment is determined by the marginal cost of labor. We know that

$$E_0^* \gtrless E_1^* + E'$$

as

$$1 + m_0^* + q(m_0^*)S^* \lessgtr 1 + m_1^* + q(m_1^*)S^*$$

This inequality states that employment will be greater in the nonsubsidized case if the marginal labor cost in that case is less than in the subsidized case. The sign of the inequality depends upon the wage premia chosen in each of the two cases. The optimal premium is that which minimizes the marginal labor cost to the firm. At that value, the effect on wages of an infinitesimal increase in the premium is just offset by the negative effect on turnover costs. In the unsubsidized case, therefore, we differentiate equation (2.2) with respect to m to derive the optimizing condition

$$1 + q'(m)S^* = 0$$

This condition is solved for m to derive m_0^*, the wage premium in the non-subsidized case; m_0^* is thus the wage premium which minimizes marginal labor costs, $1 + m + q(m)S^*$. The wage premium in the subsidized case, m_1^*, is derived by differentiating the entire expression in equation (2.2) with respect to m, setting this equal to 0 and solving for m.

Since we have shown that marginal labor costs are minimized in the unsubsidized case, it must be true that

$$1 + m_0^* + q(m_0^*)S^* < 1 + m_1^* + q(m_1^*)S^*$$

Under the subsidy, the firm optimizes in the short run by choosing a lower wage and thus a higher quit rate. Although marginal labor costs rise, the cost borne by the firm decreases because of the subsidy. This inequality implies, therefore, that $E_0^* > E_1^* + E'$.

Total employment in the unsubsidized case is greater than total employment in the subsidized case. The training subsidy thus has two direct effects. It increases the firm's per-unit profits and it shifts the composition of employment to include more disadvantaged workers. The only recommendation for such a subsidy in the short run is its presumably beneficial distributional effect.

This short-run result might certainly be modified if the firm were not operating as a perfect competitior in the labor market and were not also able to set an optimal wage premium. If, for example, the firm were a monopsonist, one could make a second-best argument that the training subsidy might induce the firm to move toward a lower marginal labor cost and thus possibly an increased employment. It is impossible to counter this argument completely, as it is always impossible to counter second-best arguments in economics. Suffice it to say that the opposite argument might be made, that the training subsidy might move the firm's equilibrium to a point even further from the minimum marginal labor cost.

Displacement in the Long Run—
A Simulation Model

The long-run displacement effects of the training subsidy provide a much more interesting case for analysis than do the short-run effects. The possibility of changes in training costs and capital stock, which are treated as decision variables in the long run, may give rise to job creation and thus to a displacement effect of less than 100 percent. We can thus use the long-run analysis to discover conditions under which the displacement effect is minimized.

We can analyze how various parameters might affect the amount of displacement and the amount of job creation that would exist for a subsidy of some constant amount. For example, the labor intensity of production might be an important factor in determining displacement. The sensitivity of the quit rate to changes in the wage rate might also affect displacement. Finally, variations in the magnitude of the extra training required might also result in differences in the amount of displacement.

These factors can be analyzed using the following model.

$$\pi = K^\alpha S^\beta \{160[E + E']\}^{1-\alpha-\beta} - 160[1 + m][E + E'] - rK$$
$$- 0.01m^{-\gamma}[E + E']S + 0.01m^{-\gamma}[g^* - \mu_g]E' \quad (2.5)$$

where r is the rental rate on capital, 160 is the number of hours worked each period by each employee, and the production function is written with the scale factor suppressed. We use a fixed amount of output and thus inquire only into the factor mix the firm uses to produce this output. Furthermore, we have made a specific assumption about the quits function—that the quit rate and the wage premium are related by a hyperbola, $q = 0.01m^{-\gamma}$, a function which satisfies the conditions of slope and convexity discussed on page 22. The sensitivity of quits to changes in wages increases as the parameter γ increases.

The firm maximizes equation (2.5) by differentiating with respect to each of the four decision variables, m, K, S, and E, and setting each of these equations equal to 0. The resulting set of equilibrium conditions is

$$m = \left\{ \frac{0.01\gamma S}{160} - \frac{0.01\gamma[g^* - \mu_g]E'}{160[E + E']} \right\}^{1/(1+\gamma)} \quad (2.6a)$$

$$S = \frac{\beta\{160[1 + m] + 0.01m^{-\gamma}S\}}{[1 - \alpha - \beta]0.01m^{-\gamma}} \quad (2.6b)$$

$$E = \frac{rK[1 - \alpha - \beta]}{\alpha\{160[1 + m] + 0.01m^{-\gamma}S\}} - E' \qquad (2.6c)$$

$$\overline{Y} = 160^{1-\alpha-\beta} K^{\alpha} S^{\beta} [E + E']^{1-\alpha-\beta} \qquad (2.6d)$$

where $\overline{Y}$ is a fixed level of output. Equation (2.6b) is derived by taking the ratio of the derivatives of equation (2.5) with respect to E and to S. Equation (2.6c) is derived analogously using the derivatives with respect to K and to E.

We want to analyze the effects of changes in the parameters α, β, γ and $[g^* - \mu_g]$ on the number of jobs created and the displacement of nonsubsidized workers which results. One way to do this would be to use implicit differentiation in the system of equations above to analyze the effects of infinitesimal shifts in these parameters. We could thus analyze what changes in the parameters cause which movements in the decision variables. Unfortunately, however, this analytical technique does not result in any determinate solution.

Since the analytical approach does not enable us to discuss the displacement problem, we shift instead to a simulation of the effects of changes in the parameters on the magnitudes of the decision variables. We report results for two values of each of the four parameters; we thus have sixteen combinations of parameters to analyze under each of three assumptions about the relation of $[g^* - \mu_g]$ to S.

The equations are set up to include production for a one-month period, and output is fixed at one million units. The training subsidy is five hundred units per month. (The only effect of changes in the subsidy's magnitude is to change the number of subsidized jobs generated.) Throughout the simulations, a rental rate on capital of 0.02 is used. The equations are solved by a modified version of the standard Gauss–Seidel iterative method in the order listed in equation (2.6). Rather than substituting the calculated value of a variable for its previous value, we instead add one-fifth of the difference between these two values to form the new value for use in the next round of iteration. This procedure was performed in order to ensure convergence. The model was simulated using additional parameter values lying between those for which the results are given. Data for these additional values are not presented because the results merely corroborate those implied by the material that follows.

Results of the Simulations

Tables 2–4 to 2–6 present the simulation results. For each of the sixteen combinations of parameters in each table we list: (1) E', the number of subsidized workers employed. (2) $E' + E_1^* - E_0^*$, the change in employment in a

Table 2–4. Subsidized Employment, Jobs Created and Percentage Displacement: Extra Training Constant

	$\beta = 0.06$			$\beta = 0.14$		
	E'	Δ Jobs	Displacement (percent)	E'	Δ Jobs	Displacement (percent)
$\alpha = 0.16$						
			$\gamma = 0.25$			
$g^* - \mu_g = 100$	190.69	0.79	99.6	245.07	0.38	99.8
$g^* - \mu_g = 500$	38.14	0.81	97.9	49.01	0.37	99.2
			$\gamma = 1.00$			
$g^* - \mu_g = 100$	45.22	3.15	93.0	139.67	1.59	98.9
$g^* - \mu_g = 500$	9.04	3.15	65.2	27.93	1.61	94.2
$\alpha = 0.40$						
			$\gamma = 0.25$			
$g^* - \mu_g = 100$	211.23	0.80	99.6	277.86	0.51	99.8
$g^* - \mu_g = 500$	42.25	0.82	98.1	55.57	0.51	99.1
			$\gamma = 1.00$			
$g^* - \mu_g = 100$	70.55	3.14	95.5	267.50	2.07	99.2
$g^* - \mu_g = 500$	14.11	3.16	77.6	53.50	2.07	96.1

Table 2–5. Subsidized Employment, Jobs Created and Percentage Displacement: Extra Training Proportional to $\sqrt{S}$

	$\beta = 0.06$			$\beta = 0.14$		
	E'	Δ Jobs	Displacement (percent)	E'	Δ Jobs	Displacement (percent)
$\alpha = 0.16$						
			$\gamma = 0.25$			
$g^* - \mu_g = \sqrt{S}$	836.8	0.79	99.9	575.3	0.43	99.9
$g^* - \mu_g = 10\sqrt{S}$	83.7	0.78	99.1	57.5	0.40	99.3
			$\gamma = 1.00$			
$g^* - \mu_g = \sqrt{S}$	394.3	3.15	99.2	394.9	1.61	99.6
$g^* - \mu_g = 10\sqrt{S}$	39.4	3.13	92.1	39.5	1.60	95.9
$\alpha = 0.40$						
			$\gamma = 0.25$			
$g^* - \mu_g = \sqrt{S}$	715.4	0.82	99.9	475.9	0.54	99.9
$g^* - \mu_g = 10\sqrt{S}$	71.5	0.81	98.9	47.6	0.54	98.9
			$\gamma = 1.00$			
$g^* - \mu_g = \sqrt{S}$	393.1	3.18	99.2	394.5	2.11	99.5
$g^* - \mu_g = 10\sqrt{S}$	39.3	3.17	91.9	39.4	2.11	94.6

Table 2–6. Subsidized Employment, Jobs Created and Percentage Displacement: Extra Training Proportional to S

	$\beta = 0.06$			$\beta = 0.14$		
	E'	Δ Jobs	Displacement (percent)	E'	Δ Jobs	Displacement (percent)
$\alpha = 0.16$						
			$\gamma = 0.25$			
$g^* - \mu_g = 0.1S$	367.19	0.80	99.8	135.06	0.41	99.7
$g^* - \mu_g = S$	36.72	0.78	97.9	13.51	0.42	96.9
			$\gamma = 1.00$			
$g^* - \mu_g = 0.1S$	343.90	3.15	99.1	111.67	1.68	98.5
$g^* - \mu_g = S$	34.39	3.14	90.6	11.17	1.67	85.0
$\alpha = 0.40$						
			$\gamma = 0.25$			
$g^* - \mu_g = 0.1S$	242.28	0.81	99.7	81.51	0.52	99.4
$g^* - \mu_g = S$	24.23	0.79	96.7	8.15	0.52	93.6
			$\gamma = 1.00$			
$g^* - \mu_g = 0.1S$	219.09	3.16	98.6	58.17	2.11	96.4
$g^* - \mu_g = S$	21.91	3.17	85.5	5.82	2.11	63.7

firm characterized by the particular combination of parameters, where E_0^* is equilibrium employment before the subsidy is given, and E_1^* is equilibrium nonsubsidized employment after the subsidy is given. And (3) the percentage displacement of nonsubsidized workers by the disadvantaged workers for whom the firm receives a training subsidy. The results in Table 2–4 are calculated under the assumption that the amount of extra training for disadvantaged workers does not vary across firms. Those in Table 2–5 are computed on the basis that the extra training is proportional to the square root of the amount of training costs. The information in Table 2–6 is calculated on the assumption that these extra costs are proportional to the training costs themselves.

Before proceeding to analyze the results under different assumptions about the parameters, we first inquire into the mechanism by which the changes in employment occur. Table 2–7 presents the solutions of the system in which no subsidy is offered, while Table 2–8 lists the results in the case in which no subsidy is given to firms and the extra training does not vary across firms. While the changes are very slight, there is a definite pattern and one which might be expected on an a priori basis. In all cases, the amount of specific training S is decreased by the subsidy, the wage premium m is lowered by the subsidy, and the quit rate is thus increased. This result is not surprising, for

Table 2–7. Values of Decision Variables in the Unsubsidized Case

| | $\beta = 0.06$ | | | | $\beta = 0.14$ | | | |
	m	K (×1000)	S	q	m	K (×1000)	S	q
				$\gamma = 0.25$				
$\alpha = 0.16$	0.0213	12,160	520.1	2.618	0.0579	12,750	1,816	2.039
$\alpha = 0.40$	0.0323	13,600	875.0	2.360	0.0959	14,330	3,415	1.797
				$\gamma = 1.00$				
$\alpha = 0.16$	0.0909	14,020	132.2	11.000	0.2800	15,290	1,254	3.572
$\alpha = 0.40$	0.1429	15,360	326.5	7.000	0.5384	17,080	4,639	1.857

Table 2–8. Values of Decision Variables in the Subsidized Case: Extra Training Constant
$(g^* - \mu_g = 100)$

| | $\beta = 0.06$ | | | | $\beta = 0.14$ | | | |
	m	K (×1000)	S	q	m	K (×1000)	S	q
				$\gamma = 0.25$				
$\alpha = 0.16$	0.0212	12,161	519.3	2.622	0.0577	12,747	1,815	2.040
$\alpha = 0.40$	0.0319	13,603	871.8	2.367	0.0954	14,329	3,409	1.800
				$\gamma = 1.00$				
$\alpha = 0.16$	0.0904	14,018	131.5	11.057	0.2793	15,285	1,251	3.580
$\alpha = 0.40$	0.1411	15,358	322.0	7.088	0.5350	17,065	4,599	1.869

the subsidy lowers the cost of turnover relative to that of wages and thus provides the firm with an incentive to increase turnover through a decline in its equilibrium m. Although the effects on these other decision variables are obviously quite minute, they are of sufficient magnitude to cause some expansion of total employment.

We shall discuss the results by analyzing the effects of changes in each of the parameters holding the other three parameters constant. Before moving to this discussion, though, one result which obtains in nearly all cases is worth discussing. Under almost all the assumptions about the relationship of the extra training to S and about the magnitudes of the parameters, the size of the percentage displacement effect is positively related to the number of subsidized workers under some fixed-budget subsidy. While the number of jobs created is in some cases positively related to the number of subsidized workers employed, in nearly every case the percentage displacement increases as the number of disadvantaged workers employed increases.

Holding the other parameters constant, an increase in the parameter α means that the labor intensity of production decreases. In three of the four combinations of β and γ in Table 2–4, the effect of an increase in α is to increase the percentage displacement. In Table 2–5, in which we assume that the extra training is proportionate to $\sqrt{S}$, there is a uniformly lesser displacement effect as production becomes more capital intensive. Similarly, in Table 2–6, in which the extra training is proportionate to S, the displacement effect becomes smaller as the capital intensity increases.

There is no apparent general effect of labor intensity on the magnitude of the displacement by subsidized workers. Unless we know the true relationship between the extra training needed to make disadvantaged workers competitive with nonsubsidized workers and the magnitude of the hiring costs, we cannot reach any specific conclusion about the effect of this production parameter α on the amount of displacement induced by the subsidy.

Variations in the specific training intensity of production, indicated by the parameter β, have different effects depending upon the assumptions made about the extra training required for disadvantaged workers. When the extra training required is constant across firms, the percentage displacement increases uniformly as the parameter β increases. If the extra training is proportionate to $\sqrt{S}$, increases in β also produce greater percentage displacement effects. In only two cases in Table 2–5 do the displacement effects not increase when the parameter β increases. If, however, the extra training requirement is proportionate to S, the result is reversed. In that case, the firm in which specific training costs are more important will be one in which the displacement effect is less.

It is apparent that the effect of the specific training intensity of production on displacement depends on the determinants of the extra training required for disadvantaged workers. If the extra training requirement increases very sharply as specific training increases, the displacement effect of increases in the training intensity of production is smaller. If the extra training required rises only slightly as specific training increases, increases in the parameter β produce more of a displacement. It is thus difficult to generalize about the effects of increasing the training intensity of production on the potential displacement effects of a training subsidy for disadvantaged workers.

The effects of a larger elasticity of substitution between S and E, σ_{SE}, on the amount of displacement can be inferred easily from our results. As σ_{SE} increases, firms can substitute raw labor for specific training more readily in response to the subsidy. (We already have shown that in all cases the subsidy induces some substitution of this type.) Thus when σ_{SE} is large, there will be a relatively large reduction in S and a relatively large increase in total employment. For any fixed-budget subsidy, the number of disadvantaged workers employed will thus be greater as σ_{SE} increases. Since we have shown that larger increases in employment of these workers produce a greater percentage displacement of nonsubsidized workers, we may conclude that the percentage displacement increases with increases in σ_{SE}.

The parameter γ measures the degree to which changes in the wage premium affect the quit rate. Unlike our discussions of the effects of the capital intensity and specific training intensity parameters, variations in the quits parameter have a uniform effect on the percentage displacement. No matter what combination of α, β, and $[g^* - \mu_g]$ is chosen, increases in γ produce a uniformly lower displacement effect. This result is especially pronounced in Table 2–4 and less so in Tables 2–5 and 2–6.

An examination of Tables 2–7 and 2–8 provides an explanation for this phenomenon. Comparing the values of m for any fixed combination of β and α, we find that the subsidy produces the same percentage decline in m at each value of the γ parameter. The elasticity of m with respect to γ is constant for different values of γ. However, considering the values of the quit rate for different values of γ but identical values of α and β, we see that the subsidy induces a substantially greater rise in the quit rate for the higher value of γ. In the case where $\alpha = 0.40$ and $\beta = 0.14$, there is an increase of only 0.003 in the quit rate when the quits parameter is 0.25. When the quits parameter rises to 1.00, the effect of the subsidy on the quit rate is 0.012. In short, the effect on turnover is greater when the quits function is more sensitive to changes in the wage rate. In that case the average labor cost borne by the firm declines more and the firm is able to expand its total employment more than if the quits function were relatively insensitive to changes in the wage rate.

A given increase in the amount of extra training required causes a proportionate decrease in the number of disadvantaged workers who can be employed for a fixed-budget subsidy. Simultaneously, though, there is no effect at all on the total employment in the firm. For that reason, the percentage displacement drops in proportion to the drop in employment among disadvantaged workers.

In conclusion, only the quit rate appears to have any effect on the percentage displacement caused by the training subsidies. Other things equal, firms in which the quit rate is higher will be ones in which the displacement effect is less. Our results also indicate that unless the occupations in which the subsidies are provided are ones in which shortages exist, policy makers face a fundamental trade-off between job creation for disadvantaged workers and the displacement of nonsubsidized workers. Not only does the absolute number of displaced workers rise as the number of placements increases;

there is also an increase in the percentage displacement of nonsubsidized workers.

Empirical Correlates of the Simulation Parameters

Since the only apparent guide to the magnitude of the potential effect is a firm's quit rate, it should be worthwhile to look at some empirical evidence on interindustry variations in the quit rate. Such an examination is especially useful if the government wishes to continue a manpower subsidy program even in the face of substantial unemployment and thus few possibilities of excess demand for specific occupations. Table 2–9 presents the average quit rate per

Table 2–9. Quit Rate and Labor Intensity for Selected Industries

Industry	Quit Rate (1967)	Labor's Share of Value Added (1967)
Metal mining	2.1	36.3
Bituminous coal and lignite mining	0.7	47.4
Lumber and wood products	4.1	57.2
Furniture and fixtures	3.7	55.0
Stone, glass, and clay products	2.3	46.1
Primary metal industries	1.4	48.8
Fabricated metal products	2.5	52.8
Machinery, except electrical	1.7	51.6
Electrical equipment and supplies	2.0	52.0
Transportation equipment	1.7	54.0
Instruments and related products	1.8	44.3
Misc. manufacturing industries	3.2	59.2
Food and kindred products	3.2	38.0
Tobacco manufactures	2.1	18.7
Textile mill products	3.4	54.9
Apparel and other textile products	2.9	56.5
Paper and allied products	2.3	45.9
Printing and publishing	2.1	51.5
Chemical and allied products	1.3	27.8
Petroleum and coal products	1.0	22.3
Rubber and plastics products, NEC	2.9	49.3
Leather and leather products	3.6	57.0
Telephone communications	1.6	51.2

Sources: (1) BLS Bulletin 1312–6, *Employment and Earnings in the United States, 1909–68.*
(2) *Statistical Abstract of the United States*, 1969, pp. 495, 666, 667, 717–721.

month for the year 1967 for each of a number of industries both in manufacturing and in other sectors. Although this series is observed at one point in
time, the relative ordering of quit rates across industries does not change
substantially during the business cycle. In general, those industries with
higher quit rates are also ones in which the wage rate is low, and are also
more likely to be located in the nondurable goods sector. Casual empiricism
suggests that services and retail trade are also characterized by relatively high
quit rates. They are, furthermore, industries in which the average level of
skill is not particularly high.

As we showed in the previous section, there is no apparent direct effect of
varying labor intensity on displacement when output is held constant. The
actual effect appeared to depend upon the assumptions about the relationship
between the amount of extra training required for disadvantaged workers and
the firm's hiring costs. If we relax our assumption that the training subsidy is
distributed randomly among firms in the economy and instead assume that
it is given to labor-intensive firms, then the total displacement effect may be
quite small. By shifting output toward more labor-intensive production, this
allocation of training funds would enable workers previously employed in the
capital-intensive sector to be absorbed in the labor-intensive sector. It is thus
important to examine what industries are in this category.

Table 2–9 exhibits labor's share of value added for each of a number of
industries. While it would be desirable to use instead an estimate of the
production parameter $[1 - \alpha - \beta]$, there are no satisfactory estimates of this
available. What few estimates do exist show substantial variability in the
parameter depending upon the time period, the data, and the estimation
procedure used.

With the exception of personal services, it is difficult to generalize about
which industries are relatively more labor-intensive. There is some vague hint
that those industries which are heavy manufacturing, such as metal products,
electrical equipment, and transportation equipment, are among those in which
production is more labor-intensive. Indeed, manufacturing as a whole is
probably one of the more labor-intensive sectors of the economy. While this
statement appears erroneous at first glance, we must remember that one
important sector has only capital as an input—the housing sector (distinct, of
course, from the construction sector). Furthermore, the government sector
with its very large stock of social overhead capital is quite likely to be more
capital-intensive than is manufacturing. Perhaps the best conclusion to be
reached on this matter is that, other things being equal and barring any
further knowledge, subsidies might be concentrated in manufacturing and
some service industries rather than in other sectors if such a concentration is
politically feasible.

The Political Dilemma

The results of our simulations imply that a real dilemma faces programs designed to increase employment for disadvantaged workers when they operate in the absence of labor-market shortages. Assuming that money under such training subsidies must be spent among all firms in the economy, the government has the choice of either increasing the number of displaced workers or decreasing the number of disadvantaged workers to be aided. This is clearly not a very appetizing choice to have to make.

One way out of this dilemma is for the government to concentrate its funds in labor-intensive industries. Aside from the political difficulties associated with such a policy, it may have some very bad implications for economic growth. In particular, it implies that the aggregate physical capital–labor ratio will decrease. If labor-intensive sectors are also those which are relatively less training-intensive, the economy will be shifted over time to a growth path in which output is growing at the same rate as before in the long run, but in which the level of output is lower than would exist if the subsidy were not applied.

If we accept the political restrictions upon the application of training subsidies in a certain area, we return to face the above policy dilemma. That this dilemma is not merely a figment of the imagination has been made apparent by statements of politicians, individual workers, and corporation executives who must deal with training programs. No less a politician than President Nixon has given cognizance to this dilemma: "As more disadvantaged Americans are being trained for jobs, the question on many working man's minds is this: 'Is that my job he's being trained to take over?' It's a direct question and a real fear. Whether reasoned or valid we all know that this fear exists, and we must deal with it head on."[24]

Public opinion polls also seem to indicate the fear which exists in the minds of lower middle-class workers who might compete directly with subsidized, disadvantaged trainees. In a poll of residents of New York City, 75 percent of the white residents questioned said they would be upset if laws were to give black workers preference for jobs.[25] It is often the case that a training subsidy for disadvantaged workers is, in effect, just such a law. This survey also indicated that preferential treatment for blacks in New York City had already reached a point where it was causing widespread resistance.[26] In Chicago, a number of workers interviewed felt that "creating jobs for blacks will cut down their own work time." As one white resident of Warren, Michigan, has noted, "The steady diet of news about the black movement and of aid for blacks makes white workers fearful their jobs are in jeopardy." These fears have been echoed by a Presidential panel studying the problems of blue-collar workers, which notes the social pressures arising from their exclusion from "programs targeted at the disadvantaged."[27]

The potential for conflict in training programs through their effects on other workers has been explicitly recognized by the Department of Labor and by corporations which receive subsidies for training. The Labor Department has instituted a series of grants to train business management in how to deal with the problems created by hiring subsidized, disadvantaged workers. As the agency describes it, "A new approach must be developed to prepare a receptive climate for this worker and [sic] his new working environment."[28] Corporation executives whose firms undertake training programs for the hard-core unemployed have been counseled about different ways of moderating the bad feelings which arise among nonsubsidized workers. Such measures as lower-than-normal compensation for trainees and their exclusion from fringe benefits have been recommended as ways of maintaining morale among existing workers. It has also become apparent that a firm involved in a subsidized training program must take into account the feelings of the union which represents the plant's workers.[29]

In times of low unemployment, the displacement caused by subsidizing disadvantaged workers may be more imaginary than real. At higher unemployment rates and when unemployment is increasing, times when labor market shortages are likely to be of minor importance, indirect displacement is a strong possibility. One form of direct displacement may even take place as nonunionized firms, seeing the subsidies offered for hiring disadvantaged workers and realizing that much of their specific investment embodied in their employees on layoff has depreciated, will choose to hire the former rather than recall the latter when product demand increases. This phenomenon is especially likely as the duration of unemployment increases, for the longer training is idle, the more it depreciates.

Even if displacement is indirect, our evidence demonstrates the fears it engenders in existing, nonsubsidized workers. They may respond to these fears by putting pressure on their elected representatives to reduce expenditures on training programs for disadvantaged workers. Although it is extremely difficult to measure the displacement effects of a specific program, it is essential that what information we have on conditions when displacement is minimized be used to modify existing training policies.

General Policies for the Goal of Maximum Jobs for Disadvantaged Individuals

It is apparent from the relationships we have outlined above that the government must do its best to minimize the displacement of nonsubsidized workers by those who qualify under the subsidy scheme. Some device must be discovered by which the discontent on the part of the displaced workers is minimized so that it does not feed back to the appropriations process for the training program. In this section we consider two general changes which would increase the amount of appropriations available in the long run for training disadvantaged workers.

Given the desire to employ disadvantaged workers in jobs where they are not presently able to be hired, policy could be aimed at minimizing the displacement caused by a given number of such workers. Training policy should be much more conscious than it now is about whether a true shortage exists in the occupation in which training is offered. The government can, for example, adopt a policy of not providing training subsidies at times when the unemployment rate reaches some specific level. When the unemployment rate is very high, it is safe to assume that the number of occupations in which excess demand exists is comparatively small. Given this lack of excess demand for labor, the model we have outlined above becomes perfectly applicable. Its results show that in such a case the amount of displacement is likely to be very high. Rather than risk discontent which might arise from sending non-subsidized workers out into the labor market in times of low aggregate demand, the government might well save up its money to subsidize trainees at times in which demand is more substantial. In Chapter 6 we outline a specific program designed to meet this objection to current policy.

Even when the unemployment rate is low, manpower planners should not rely upon lists of occupations in which scarcities exist. As we discussed earlier, the unwillingness of many firms to participate is such that these lists are likely to be poor indicators of the areas in which trainees can be placed without displacing other workers. Instead, the authorities in charge of such a program, in the United States the State Training and Employment Services, should make much more frequent surveys of job conditions in the labor markets under their charge. While such an information-gathering program might be fairly expensive, frequent surveys are essential if training subsidies are to be more than merely redistributive devices.

If shortages are of similar magnitudes in two occupations, our results show that subsidies should be applied to that occupation in which the quit rate is likely to be higher, i.e., where, in general, the less-skilled jobs are. Application of subsidy money in this manner would do much to prevent displacement of nonsubsidized workers. There is a long-run problem of concentrating money in this area, for technological change may decrease the potential for promotion out of these less-skilled jobs. Nonetheless, as a middle-run policy, concentration of the training subsidy in certain occupations may have beneficial effects on the total amount of funds that can be appropriated for training disadvantaged workers.

In addition to avoiding displacement, manpower planners also have the option of trying to increase the effectiveness of fixed-budget subsidies in increasing employment among workers at whom the subsidy is aimed. In terms of the model outlined in this chapter this policy would imply an attempt to lower $[g^* - \mu_g]$, the extra profits earned by the firm on workers who are not the least able workers being subsidized by the program. Some attempt could be made to avoid the "creaming" that now takes place in training programs and thus shift the benefits of the program toward the most needy workers.

Even if the economic goal is solely that of helping previously disadvantaged citizens, it behooves the makers of manpower policy to consider the potential displacement effects of that policy. On economic grounds, it hardly makes sense to create one group of unemployed workers in place of another, slightly less fortunate group. On political grounds, unless displacement is minimized, our discussion indicates that the funds available for future manpower subsidies will be diminished. Finally, on equity grounds, it is only fair to lower middle-class citizens that they not be required to bear the economic burden of aiding less-fortunate members of society.

3

Alternative Subsidies for Depressed Areas

Policy designed to ameliorate conditions in depressed areas of the United States has not recognised possible differences in their characteristics. There has been little serious consideration of what distinguishes these labor markets from one another. In this chapter, we will discuss a number of possible subsidies which can be given to depressed areas and the labor market characteristics which make them more or less desirable. Subsidies for training labor and for hiring labor have both been used to increase the employment of idle human resources. Capital subsidies in the form of guaranteed loans and government loan participation have also been used for the stated purpose of providing employment for workers in depressed areas. Migration subsidies are also a possibility that might be feasible when other measures prove too expensive. However, because their purpose differs from that of the other subsidies discussed and because of the political difficulties inherent in removing constituents from a legislator's district, we ignore them in our discussion.[1]

The Goal of Aiding Depressed Areas

The economic problems of chronically depressed areas in which unemployment remains well above the national average were recognised as early as 1955 by advisors to the United States government.

Local unemployment often proves stubborn when it stems from special causes, such as a dwindling market for the products in which a community has specialized, the removal of one or more of its key firms to other places, a lag in the technology of its principal industry, or the depletion of a natural resource on which the local economy is based.[2]

The realization that such area differentials in unemployment were not transitory, and a change in the political composition of the government, led in 1961 to the passage of the Area Redevelopment Act. This measure explicitly stated that "the federal government should help areas with substantial and persistent unemployment and underemployment to take effective steps in planning and financing their economic redevelopment."[3] The goal of both

43

the capital and labor subsidies offered under this act is chiefly that of reducing unemployment localized in certain areas.

Regional development policy has by no means been used solely in the United States. Great Britain has for a long time been involved in substantial subsidization in so-called " development areas." These efforts took an innovative turn in 1967 with the introduction of the Regional Employment Premium, a wage subsidy for every hour of labor paid for by manufacturing firms in the development area. Its goal was stated to be that of securing "a further substantial narrowing of the unemployment gap between the development areas and the rest of Britain."[4] Canada also recognized the importance of this goal and linked it both to rapid economic growth and to the attainment of full employment with reasonable price stability.[5]

The goal of raising standards in depressed areas up to those in the rest of the nation has long been valued in a number of developed countries. Indeed, in the United States this goal was the first one for which federally sponsored manpower training was proposed. Training toward achieving this goal is aimed not at a particular segment of a labor market, but rather at all workers in the labor market of what is designated as a depressed area.

The Nature of the Labor Market in a Depressed Area

By inference we must assume that the wage in a depressed area is downward rigid at the going wage rate. If not, unemployed workers would compete among themselves for available jobs, lower the wage rate and remove the existing unemployment. This does not happen, as evidenced by the continuing high unemployment. Thus, in the remainder of this chapter, we will make the assumption that there is some minimum wage which each individual must receive in order to work at a job for which he has been trained. While there is some migration out of depressed areas, this process is very slow and does not appear to remove much of the persistent unemployment. For our purpose, therefore, we shall assume that, with the exception of mobility in response to migration subsidies, the labor market we are discussing is closed, i.e., there are no flows in or out. This assumption allows us to abstract from possible inflows of workers attracted by subsidies which are not structured administratively to avoid this problem.

The assumptions made above about the nature of labor markets in depressed areas are fairly reasonable ones, but they do not explain the underlying reasons for depression in individual areas. The diversity of reasons is much too great to be encompassed by one or even several explanations. This multiplicity of causes and the location of labor markets which qualify as depressed are illustrated by the data in Table 3–1. For each state we list: (1) The number of counties in major labor market areas in which there is persistent unemployment. (2) The number of counties in all such major areas. (3) The number of counties in smaller labor areas with persistent unemployment. And (4) the total number of counties not included under (2).

Table 3–1. Counties in Labor Markets with Persistent Unemployment, and Total Counties, September 1969

	(1)/(2)[a] Major[b] Areas	(3)/(4) Smaller Areas		(1)/(2) Major Areas	(3)/(4) Smaller Areas
Alabama	0/5	4/61	Montana	0/0	5/56
Alaska[c]	0/0	22/24	Nebraska	0/3	0/90
Arizona	0/1	3/13	Nevada	0/0	1/17
Arkansas	0/2	12/72	New Hampshire[d]	0/4	0/234
California	2/15	28/43	New Jersey	0/10	1/6
Colorado	0/5	2/58	New Mexico	0/1	10/31
Connecticut[d]	0/66	0/103	New York	0/27	12/36
Delaware	0/3	0/2	North Carolina	0/7	17/93
Florida	0/4	4/63	North Dakota	0/0	1/53
Georgia	0/13	23/147	Ohio	0/29	10/64
Hawaii	0/1	0/4	Oklahoma	0/6	20/71
Idaho	0/0	6/44	Oregon	0/4	13/33
Illinois	0/14	12/89	Pennsylvania	0/28	4/42
Indiana	0/20	9/70	Rhode Island[d]	0/40	0/8
Iowa	0/2	1/95	South Carolina	0/4	7/41
Kansas	0/2	0/101	South Dakota	0/0	0/67
Kentucky	0/3	51/114	Tennessee	0/10	13/87
Louisiana	0/7	20/57	Texas	0/21	17/233
Maine[d]	0/9	79/487	Utah	0/1	11/28
Maryland	0/6	4/15	Vermont[d]	0/0	0/251
Massachusetts[d]	6/159	39/196	Virginia	0/13	11/110
Michigan	0/15	37/67	Washington	0/4	8/34
Minnesota	0/6	21/82	West Virginia	0/8	35/48
Mississippi	0/2	10/80	Wisconsin	0/6	10/65
Missouri	0/13	12/106	Wyoming	0/0	0/23

Sources: Manpower Administration, *Area Trends in Employment and Unemployment*, September 1969, pp. 5–14; Manpower Administration, *Directory of Important Labor Areas*, October 1967; and Bureau of the Census, *Census of Population, 1960*, PC(1)C, volumes for each state.
[a] See text for definition of (1), (2), (3), and (4). State totals do not necessarily equal true number of counties or towns because some major areas are defined to include jurisdictions in several states.
[b] Major areas correspond to Standard Metropolitan Statistical Areas.
[c] Election districts.
[d] Towns and incorporated cities.

The data are for September 1969, a time of extremely low unemployment nationwide (3.8 percent), yet the areas in the table had unemployment rates greater than 6 percent for periods greater than one year. Some areas, such as the agricultural counties in California, have large proportions of very low-skilled migrant laborers. In other areas, especially the old bituminous coal mining counties of Kentucky and West Virginia, labor has been displaced by the mechanization of production of the areas' major products. Still other areas, such as the iron mining country of northern Michigan and Minnesota, are places hurt by the depletion of a natural resource. Other areas listed in the table are those which have been damaged by the failure of a local company to remain competitive. In some cases, particularly those of the New England textile towns, this decline is due to competition from both foreign and domestic sources. That all of these areas might still be considered depressed in 1969 is illustrative of the difficulties involved in adjusting to the decline in demand for a local product.

It is clear from the table that most of what qualify as depressed areas in the United States are rural and small-town areas. Only three of the 147 major labor markets had persistent unemployment, and even these (Fresno and Stockton, California; and New Bedford, Massachusetts) were among the smallest of the major areas. In discussing policy we must thus remember that we are implicitly ignoring policies which might help a nation's urban problems and concentrating instead on small, isolated areas.

Depressed areas in Canada are qualitatively different from those in the United States. In this country, many of the areas which qualify as depressed are located between the major centers of industry. For example, the coal mining areas in Kentucky and West Virginia are near the major markets of the mid-Atlantic area. In Canada, this situation is different; for the Atlantic provinces, the largest depressed area in the country, lie far from the major industrial areas of Ontario and Quebec. It is essential that these differences be recognized so that policy for depressed areas can be implemented rationally. Surely the possible success of different types of subsidies depends upon the location of the area relative to major markets. These differences should, therefore, be considered in prescribing subsidies designed to improve the employment situation in the depressed area.

Training vs. Wage Subsidies in the Short Run

In this section, we compare two of the subsidies which have been given to raise employment in areas of persistent high unemployment. Our analysis has the additional benefit of providing a general model of the firm's decisions about employment, wages, and turnover. The model we use is similar to that presented in Chapter 2, except that here all untrained labor is assumed to be homogeneous, i.e., the firm's training costs are identical for all workers.

We assume without loss of generality that the supply of unskilled labor to the firm is perfectly elastic at a wage equal to one. Moreover, we assume that all untrained labor is homogeneous and that after being trained the skills of employed workers become differentiated from those of the unemployed. All training is assumed to take place in one time period; this assumption is not very restrictive, for the unit of time can be defined to be arbitrarily long to accommodate any required training period. For purposes of simplification we will assume that there are no dropouts from the training process. This assumption could be modified to make the dropout rate dependent on the wage the worker will receive in the firm after he is trained relative to the wage he could get elsewhere. Such a modification would in no way alter the results in this section.

The analysis is restricted in this section to the short run, so that the capital stock and the amount of training per worker are assumed fixed. In the short run, only training and wage subsidies are relevant, for the assumption of fixed capital obviates the need to discuss investment subsidies. Since the neoclassical short-run production function includes capital as a fixed factor, it seems reasonable to expand the short run and assume that the amount of training required for workers to use that capital is also fixed. Viewed differently, this assumption is that the training process involves fixed routines which cannot be changed very rapidly. An extreme example of this short-run complementarity of fixed capital and fixed training is provided by pilot training procedures for military aircraft. A rigid prescription of ground training, accompanied flight, and solo flight exists, and this routine differs among individual aircraft.

The crucial assumption of this section is its use of Becker's distinction between general and specific training.[6] The firm trains workers in some skills which are applicable in other firms and invests some money which raises the worker's productivity only in the individual firm. We assume that the required expenditures on general training are G^* and those on specific training are S^*. Following Becker's argument, we assume that the worker pays for the entire costs of his general training by accepting a wage less than the unskilled wage during the training period. Specific training costs are borne by the firm and include the worker's wage during the training process (which is assumed to take up all his time during the training period). As in Chapter 2 we have both m, the premium over the unskilled wage rate, and employment, E, as the firm's decision variables in the short run.

We proceed to calculate the direct employment effects of each of the two subsidies in the firm which receives the subsidy. The firm facing an across-the-board (area-wide) wage or training subsidy seeks to maximize

$$\pi = f(E) - [1 + m - c]E - q(m)E[S^* - t] \qquad (3.1)$$

where

$$c = \text{dollar-amount wage subsidy}$$
$$t = \text{dollar-amount training subsidy}$$

and $f(E)$ is the short-run production function whose first two derivatives alternate in sign; $q(m)$ is the same quits function used in Chapter 2; and the price of the product is assumed to be exogenous and equal to one. Both the wage and training subsidies apply to all workers hired and employed by the firm selected to receive them. The model is thus directly applicable to the analysis of policies designed to aid an entire depressed area.

The general profit-maximizing conditions are

$$\frac{\partial \pi}{\partial m} = 1 + q'(m)[S^* - t] = 0 \qquad (3.2)$$

and

$$\frac{\partial \pi}{\partial E} = f'(E) - [1 + m - c] - q(m)[S^* - t] = 0 \qquad (3.3)$$

Equation (3.2) states that the firm will set a wage premium m such that the increase in direct wage costs resulting from a slight increase in m is just offset by the decrease in replacement costs. Equation (3.3) states that the marginal product of labor will be set equal to the wage plus the replacement cost of training.[7]

What happens to the wage premium and employment in this profit-maximizing firm when the government offers it subsidies aimed at increasing its employment? The solutions for the decision variables are

$$m^* = q'^{-1}\left(\frac{-1}{S^* - t}\right) \qquad (3.4)$$

and

$$E^* = f'^{-1}\big([1 + m^* - c] + q(m^*)[S^* - t]\big) \qquad (3.5)$$

Since the derivative of the function q'^{-1} is positive, it can be shown by differentiating in (3.4) and (3.5) that the derivatives of E^* with respect to c and t are both positive and that

$$\frac{\partial m^*}{\partial c} = 0 \qquad \frac{\partial m^*}{\partial t} < 0$$

The dollar-amount wage subsidy has no effect on wages because it does not change the terms on which the firm trades off between direct wage costs and turnover costs. The dollar-amount training subsidy makes training relatively cheaper and induces the firm to pay a lower wage at the cost of a higher quit rate and more frequent need to incur the reduced costs of training.

Assume we give subsidies that generate E_f total employment in the firm, an amount higher than the firm's employment before it received the subsidy. We inquire into the costs of the two subsidies in producing this additional employment in the particular firm. For the wage and training subsidies respectively they are

$$C_1 = cE_f \tag{3.6}$$

and

$$C_2 = tq(m_2^*)E_f \tag{3.7}$$

where m_2^* is the premium paid by the firm under the training subsidy. Since each subsidy is to produce an equal level of employment, E_f, the argument of f'^{-1} in equation (3.5), must be the same under both subsidies

$$1 + m_1^* - c + q(m_1^*)S^* = 1 + m_2^* + q(m_2^*)[S^* - t] \tag{3.8}$$

where m_1^* is the wage premium under the wage subsidy (and in the free-market case as well). Solving for c in equation (3.8) and substituting in (3.6) we have

$$C_1 = E_f\{[m_1^* - m_2^*] + [q(m_1^*) - q(m_2^*)]S^* + tq(m_2^*)S^*\} \tag{3.9}$$

We subtract equation (3.7) from equation (3.9) to derive

$$C_1 - C_2 = E_f\{[m_1^* - m_2^*] + [q(m_1^*) - q(m_2^*)]S^*\} \tag{3.10}$$

If we apply the mean value theorem to equation (3.10) we have

$$C_1 - C_2 = E_f\{[m_1^* - m_2^*][1 + q'(m_k)S^*]\} \qquad m_1^* > m_k > m_2^* \tag{3.11}$$

Under the wage subsidy alone equation (3.2) states that

$$1 + q'(m_1^*)S^* = 0$$

Since $m_k < m_1^*$ and $q'' > 0$

$$1 + q'(m_k)S^* < 0$$

so that the expression in equation (3.11) must be negative. In order to make (3.11) comparable with the results to be derived later in this section, we rewrite it by subtracting zero in the form of $E_f[m_1^* - m_2^*][1 + q'(m_1^*)S^*]$

$$C_1 - C_2 = E_f\{[m_1^* - m_2^*][q'(m_k) - q'(m_1^*)]S^*\} \qquad (3.12)$$

The across-the-board wage subsidy is thus uniformly more efficient in raising employment in the firms receiving the subsidies. It is more efficient because it does not alter the ratio of wages paid, $[1 + m]$, to training costs, $q(m)S^*$, from its free-market value. The dollar-amount training subsidy does lower the wage, but the decrease in average direct wage costs is less than the increase in average replacement costs.

One could modify this analysis to make the effective specific training fixed at S^* but have actual expenditures on training be a decreasing function of the wage paid by the firm. The rationale for this is that higher wages bring an increased flow of applicants to the firm and thus lower the costs of search for new workers. Furthermore, these applicants may be more easily trainable. As can be seen by substituting $S(m)$ for S^* in equation (3.1) and deriving the new profit-maximizing conditions, this modification does not change the result that the wage subsidy leaves unchanged the wages paid by the firm. Since the training subsidy does change the wage paid, this complication of the model in no way affects our conclusion that the wage subsidy is more efficient in producing a direct employment increase in the subsidized firm in which training is entirely specific.

In addition to the direct increase in employment in the firms receiving the subsidies, society benefits in future periods from the general training which workers have received. This training, insofar as it does not become obsolete and is applied in firms where it can be of use, saves workers the costs of investment in general training in future periods. That is, during the initial period of employment after they have quit the subsidized firm, workers who have received general training need not forego wages to pay for all of the general training required in these jobs. Unlike the case of the direct effect, this indirect effect is greater for the training than for the wage subsidy.

Consider the expenditures on the subsidy during a single time period in a labor market in which the subsidy has been given for a long time. During this period some of the E_f employees quit, releasing into the economy of this labor market G^* of general training per man which may be useful in other firms. The difference in the total number of men released during this period under the wage as opposed to the training subsidy is

$$[q(m_1^*) - q(m_2^*)]E_f \qquad (3.13)$$

Our problem is to determine the value of this general training by inquiring into how much future investment in general training has been saved by the investment in workers who quit. We assume that there is no obsolescence of general training; that all the general training given by the subsidized firm can be used by other firms in which the workers will be employed; and that there is no period of unemployment between jobs. The result we derive is thus a limiting condition, for these three assumptions, especially the last of them, are not strictly applicable.[8] As will become apparent below, they bias our results in favour of preferring the training subsidy over the wage subsidy.

The average worker who quits the firm receiving the wage subsidy has been employed for $1/q(m_1^*)$ periods. In the case of the training subsidy the comparable figure is $1/q(m_2^*)$, a somewhat shorter duration of employment. These two figures are the points at which the subsidized worker begins to use his earlier general training in other jobs. In his new job he does not have to forego any earnings to pay for his general training, for the training is already embodied in him. These two points in time are the periods when future investment in general training is saved; they should thus be used in discounting the benefits of the alternative subsidies.

Given our assumption that all of the general training is used and that there is no period intervening between the time the worker quits the subsidized firm and the time he is hired elsewhere, the discounted value of the general training per worker is

$$G^* \exp\left(-\frac{\rho}{q(m_1^*)}\right)$$

for the wage subsidy, and

$$G^* \exp\left(-\frac{\rho}{q(m_2^*)}\right)$$

for the training subsidy. (The parameter ρ is the discount rate used by the government in evaluating its manpower projects.) Only the savings on training expenditures in the worker's first job after he quits the subsidized firm are attributed to the subsidy program. It is debatable whether the savings on training in additional jobs in the future should be counted. We do not count them here, for this secondary saving would exist if the worker had been hired by an unsubsidized firm and had then left that firm to work elsewhere. In any event this neglect does not qualitatively change our results.

The difference in the total discounted benefits produced by the two subsidies is

$$B_1 - B_2 = G^* E_f \left\{ q(m_1^*) \exp\left(-\frac{\rho}{q(m_1^*)} \right) - q(m_2^*) \exp\left(-\frac{\rho}{q(m_2^*)} \right) \right\} \quad (3.14)$$

Using the mean value theorem to make equation (3.14) comparable to equation (3.12), we have

$$B_1 - B_2 = G^* E_f [m_1^* - m_2^*] q'(m_l) \exp\left(-\frac{\rho}{q(m_l)} \right) \left[1 + \frac{\rho}{q(m_l)} \right]$$

$$m_1^* > m_l > m_2^* \quad (3.15)$$

which, given our assumptions about the shape of $q(m)$, is strictly negative.

The reduction in future expenditures on general training by workers in the form of reduced wages during the future training period is greater for the training subsidy. Since this type of subsidy has the effect of lowering wages and increasing the quit rate, it produces a greater number of generally trained workers who leave the firm looking for other jobs. Its superiority in the production of these trained workers increases as the quits function becomes more responsive to changes in the wage premium and as the social discount rate increases.

If the worker receives general training throughout his tenure in the subsidized firm, this result is no longer valid. The wage subsidy, because it increases the average duration of employment, would increase the amount of general training received. This result is one more reason why the decision rule we derive is a limiting condition which is biased in favor of the across-the-board training subsidy.

We can compare the lower cost of the wage subsidy in producing increased employment in the subsidized firm to the greater discounted saving on future investment in general training which the training subsidy produces. These two quantities are expressed in terms of value during the initial period when a cohort of workers is hired, and they are thus quite comparable. They allow us to combine in one piece of analysis the two policy goals of increasing the stock of general training and increasing employment in the area.

The difference between the two programs in the costs of producing the direct increase in employment is given by equation (3.12), while the difference in the value of the indirect effects is supplied by equation (3.15). If we consider these equations, the wage subsidy (WS) is more efficient than the training subsidy (TS) or vice versa

$$WS \gtreqless TS \quad \text{as} \quad B_1 - B_2 \gtreqless C_1 - C_2 \tag{3.16}$$

Substituting equations (3.12) and (3.15) into equation (3.16) and rearranging, we obtain

$$WS \gtreqless TS \quad \text{as} \quad \frac{S^*}{G^*} \gtreqless \frac{q'(m_l) \exp\left(-\dfrac{\rho}{q(m_l)}\right)\left[1 + \dfrac{\rho}{q(m_l)}\right]}{[q'(m_k) - q'(m_1^*)]} \tag{3.17}$$

One should note that, because of our assumptions about the usefulness of the general training provided by the subsidized firm, the condition in equation (3.17) is a limiting condition. If it shows a wage subsidy to be more efficient, we can be certain the result is correct. If, however, the training subsidy appears dominant, it may not be so in actuality. Each side of the inequality in (3.17) is nonnegative, so that the question of which subsidy is preferred depends crucially on the relative amounts of the two classes of training provided by the subsidized firm. As the training becomes more specific and less general, the wage subsidy increases in desirability. Indeed, in the case of purely specific training the wage subsidy is uniformly most efficient.

To apply the decision rule one must determine the relative magnitudes of the required training in individual firms or classes of firms, perhaps by relating them to observed characteristics of the firm. Some estimates of the hiring-cost component of specific training were presented in Table 2–3. They indicate, as would be expected, that hiring costs increase with the skill level of a firm's employees. There are, unfortunately, no available data on the general-training content of training by skill level, so that it is difficult to draw any conclusion about the correlation between skill level and the mix of required training. Suffice it to say that the empirical determination of this and other correlations between the training mix and variables characterizing different firms has been almost completely neglected and is important for policy.

As can be seen by differentiating with respect to ρ in equation (3.17), the right-hand side increases as ρ increases. If a higher discount rate is used by manpower planners, the training subsidy becomes a more desirable means of increasing employment in depressed labor markets. Our results thus demonstrate that the magnitude of the social discount rate should also be an important criterion to use in discriminating between the relative merits of alternative subsidies.

While we have no objective predictions about which type of subsidy is more desirable in which firm or industry, this analysis does make several points clear. Subsidies which aim to increase training and employment, whether called wage or training subsidies, are economically equivalent. Each reduces the firm's average labor costs and each operates to increase employment in the subsidized firm and to increase the likelihood of future employment for workers who quit that firm. More important, our result suggests that there is no need for manpower policy to rely exclusively on either across-the-board wage or training subsidies. Rather, a government should tailor the subsidies it offers to the nature of training and employment in the particular firm receiving the subsidy. Firms which spend relatively much on specific training and on searching for new workers should be singled out to receive the wage rather than the training subsidy.

While our result deals with polar cases, any combination of subsidies can also be fitted into our analysis. For example, a program which both places workers and pays part of their wages during their employment is a mixed wage-training subsidy, for the firm is saved part of the initial costs of search for new workers. Our result can be applied to such a program simply by weighting equations (3.12) and (3.15) by the relative expenditures of the program on wages and on training.

Training vs. Wage Subsides in the Long Run

In the foregoing section, we assumed that both the amount of general and specific training was fixed and the amount of capital could also not be varied. In this section, we relax these assumptions and move toward a longer time horizon. We inquire into the degree to which this change affects the desirability of the subsidies discussed above. We assume here that the firm's output is constant, so that we are only concerned with how factor proportions change. This assumption is relaxed in the discussion in the next section. The firm's decision variables in the model here are the same as those in the simulation model of Chapter 2: employment, capital, the wage premium, and the amount of specific training per employee.

Although we considered general training as being fixed in the short run, one can argue that we need not view it as being a decision variable for the firm in the long run. Since general training neither produces a return for the firm nor is paid for by the firm, the profit-maximizing firm will provide an indeterminate amount of general training in the long run. Presumably the amount of general training actually offered depends upon some complementarity with the amount of specific training the firm desires to provide in order to maximize its profits. Because of this complementarity and because general training does not enter the firm's profit-maximizing condition, we assume that it can be ignored in the consideration of the effects of alternative subsidies in the long run.

In the previous section we considered only the dollar-amount wage and training subsidies. Our discussion was restricted to these because a percentage training subsidy is analytically identical to the dollar-amount training subsidy in the short run. The percentage wage subsidy does present different results from the dollar-amount subsidy; we ignored it before merely for the sake of expositional simplicity. (Compared to the dollar-amount wage subsidy the percentage wage subsidy produces results different from those of the training subsidy; i.e., in this comparison, the dollar wage subsidy always dominates in the short run.) In this section we consider all four subsidies, and we specify them as

$$\$WS = cE \qquad\qquad \$TS = tq(m)E$$
$$\%WS = x[1 + m]E \qquad \%TS = \tau Sq(m)E$$

where c and t are as in equation (3.1), x is the parameter describing the percentage of the wage bill subsidized by the government, and τ is the parameter describing the percentage of training and hiring costs subsidized by the government. All of these are subsidies *to the firm* based upon the wages it pays or the training it offers.

In the general case in which all four subsidies are included, the firm maximizes

$$\pi = K^\alpha S^\beta [160E]^{1-\alpha-\beta} - 160[1 + m - c][1 - x]$$
$$\times E - rK - 0.01m^{-\gamma}[S - t][1 - \tau]E$$
$$(3.18)$$

where r is the rate of return on capital. We have included in this maximization the same specification of the quits function and the same hours per employee as were included in Chapter 2. In the actual analysis, of course, we consider three of the four subsidy parameters as being zero and discuss the results in the case in which the fourth one is nonzero.

We wish to consider the effects on the values of the endogenous variables, in particular the values of S and E, of spending identical amounts through each of the four subsidies. In this case it is clear that the answers cannot be provided through mathematical analysis. We know that both wage subsidies will increase employment, so the mere presentation of directions of change will not provide us with any answers. We must instead use the numerical methods outlined in Chapter 2 to solve for the endogenous variables under each of the alternative subsidies.

In Table 3–2 we present the values of each of the four endogenous variables as well as of the quit rate resulting from the wage premium in each case. The parameters which vary in each simulation are α, the capital intensity of production; β, the training-cost intensity of production; and γ, the slope of the quits function. For each of the eight possible combinations of these parameters we list the values of the endogenous variables in the unsubsidized case (NS), as well as their values under each of the four alternative subsidies.

A careful reading of Table 3–2 suggests that there is a trade-off between increased employment and increased amounts of training. Within each combination of simulation parameters the highest employment is produced by that subsidy which produces simultaneously the lowest amount of per capita training expenditures. This result suggests that if the goal of manpower policy in depressed areas is to produce the maximum employment, it will do so at the cost of producing a less well-trained work force. This cost must be considered, and perhaps the goal should be modified to include some combination of desired training embodied in workers and desired increases in employment.

In the short-run case, the dollar-amount training subsidy produced a smaller direct increase in employment in a given firm for a fixed cost than did the dollar-amount wage subsidy. In the long run, however, this subsidy ranks first among the four considered in producing increases in employment in the firm being subsidized. The subsidy induces the firm to decrease its wage premium drastically, producing a very large increase in the turnover rate. In addition, the firm decreases per capita training expenditures as well as decreasing its capital input. (This latter decrease occurs under all four subsidies in each of the eight parameter combinations.) The reason for the surprising reversal of results must be that this subsidy is not linked to the amount of training the firm provides. It therefore pays the profit-maximizing firm to increase its turnover and increase its steady state employment so as to receive the maximum amount of subsidy. One way of doing this is to lower the amount of training embodied in workers, resulting in increased turnover and a concomitant increase in the amount of subsidy received.

The dollar-amount wage subsidy ranks second in producing increases in employment; the percentage wage subsidy ranks third; and the percentage training subsidy ranks fourth. Indeed, this last subsidy always produces a

Table 3–2. Simulation Results, Across-the-Board Subsidies

	β = 0.06					β = 0.14				
	S	E	m	K	q	S	E	m	K	q
α = 0.16			γ = 0.25					γ = 0.25		
NS	520.1	6697.9	0.0213	12,161	2.618	1815.7	6025.3	0.0578	12,748	2.039
$WS	516.8	6706.9	0.0212	12,120	2.622	1802.1	6032.7	0.0575	12,695	2.042
%WS	517.1	6706.7	0.0213	12,120	2.619	1805.2	6031.6	0.0578	12,697	2.039
$TS	509.4	6712.8	0.0200	12,125	2.659	1792.1	6035.1	0.0563	12,697	2.053
%TS	548.5	6676.6	0.0213	12,117	2.619	1854.7	6015.9	0.0578	12,729	2.039
α = 0.40										
NS	875.0	1976.6	0.0323	13,602	2.360	3414.5	1634.7	0.0959	14,331	1.797
$WS	858.5	1992.9	0.0318	13,500	2.369	3337.2	1650.7	0.0942	14,200	1.805
%WS	862.2	1991.9	0.0323	13,500	2.359	3359.8	1648.9	0.0960	14,210	1.797
$TS	825.5	2002.1	0.0277	13,499	2.451	3274.0	1656.3	0.0890	14,176	1.831
%TS	983.0	1961.4	0.0323	13,498	2.360	3580.9	1629.0	0.0958	14,286	1.798
α = 0.16			γ = 1.00					γ = 1.00		
NS	132.3	7227.7	0.0909	14,019	10.998	1254.0	5972.4	0.2799	15,288	3.572
$WS	130.9	7239.4	0.0904	13,978	11.063	1237.3	5982.3	0.2779	15,226	3.599
%WS	131.4	7235.0	0.0907	13,973	11.023	1244.1	5981.1	0.2791	15,238	3.582
$TS	123.9	7267.1	0.0859	13,976	11.637	1201.3	6000.9	0.2712	15,193	3.687
%TS	138.5	7205.3	0.0909	13,977	11.002	1281.0	5962.2	0.2803	15,278	3.567
α = 0.40										
NS	326.6	2015.7	0.1429	15,358	6.998	4636.5	1387.7	0.5383	17,076	1.858
$WS	317.2	2033.2	0.1409	15,256	7.098	4455.5	1404.2	0.5281	16,917	1.894
%WS	322.8	2029.4	0.1431	15,257	6.988	4570.3	1398.0	0.5384	16,954	1.857
$TS	273.1	2065.3	0.1232	15,258	8.115	4041.3	1426.3	0.4914	16,782	2.035
%TS	362.8	2002.1	0.1431	15,259	6.990	4847.1	1382.6	0.5392	17,039	1.855

decline in employment compared to its value in the unsubsidized case. This result is not surprising, for the amount of subsidy the firm receives is directly linked to the amount of training it offers. The profit-maximizing firm will, therefore, increase the amount of training provided in order to increase the amount of subsidy received. The ranking of the four subsidies is identical under all combinations of the simulation parameters. While the relative amounts of increased employment and decreased training expenditures per capita vary across these parameter combinations, the ordinal rankings remain the same.

It appears that if the sole aim of the government in its manpower policies for depressed areas is that of increasing employment, it should rely exclusively on dollar-amount training subsidies. In other words, it should make grants of fixed amounts to individual firms in depressed areas for each worker they hire. If, on the other hand, the goal is that of increasing the amount of training embodied in workers, subsidies should be geared to the amount of training provided by the firm. Since it is extremely difficult to measure this quantity, the actual operation of the percentage-training subsidy is not quite so simple as that of the dollar-amount training subsidy. One method might be to give a larger subsidy to those firms having a smaller turnover rate. Since, in the long run, the turnover rate is negatively correlated with the amount of training provided by the firm, this method of subsidy should produce the desired increase in training expenditures by firms.[9]

If the government wishes to increase employment while reducing training expenditures by firms as little as possible, the policy to follow is some type of wage subsidy. In all of the simulations, the differences between the dollar-amount and the percentage wage subsidies are minute, so that the choice between these two alternatives is a matter of indifference. The similarity in the results produced by each of these suggests that the actual policy choice should depend chiefly on the relative costs of administering each of them.

Capital Subsidies to Increase Employment

In our simulations above, we held the firm's output fixed. Under this condition a capital subsidy to firms would produce an increase in the capital stock and a decrease both in employment and the amount of training per capita, given our assumptions about the nature of the production function. In this section, we relax the assumption of constant output and inquire into conditions under which a capital subsidy would be more or less likely to produce increases in employment. It may even be that in some cases a capital subsidy would be more efficacious than some types of labor subsidies in producing such increases. Of course, it has the detrimental effect of shifting a mobile resource, physical capital, to an inefficient use.[10]

Our interest in capital subsidies stems from the observation that the large majority of regional subsidies are of this variety. They are usually given in order to meet the goal of reducing unemployment in depressed areas and they are sometimes of quite large magnitude. It behooves us, therefore, to consider what parameters will affect the success of these subsidies.

The actual amount of capital subsidies varies among developed countries offering this type of program. In Canada, for example, the government spent approximately $370 million on this program in the years 1963–1967.[11] This compares extremely favorably on a per-capita basis with the efforts of the United States government. Including both the ARA and its successor, the Economic Development Act, total federal expenditures in the form of both grants and loans were slightly under $900 million for the years 1961 through 1969.[12] Despite the presence of depressed areas in an otherwise prosperous economy, the United States' effort at improving conditions in them has been on a relatively small scale given the size of its population.

Perhaps the most important parameter likely to affect the success of capital subsidies to firms in reducing unemployment is the elasticity of supply of capital to particular depressed areas. If the supply elasticity is greater, a subsidy reducing the effective interest rate paid by firms would have a substantially greater effect in drawing in new capital to a particular area. Because of the complementarity of capital and labor this would in turn produce a larger increase in employment, assuming that the production parameters in any two areas being compared are identical. An important consideration affecting the decision whether capital subsidies or employment subsidies are to be offered should thus be the supply elasticity of capital to the depressed area.

One major factor affecting this elasticity is likely to be the nearness and accessability of the depressed area to product markets. If transport costs are not very important, a capital subsidy should sharply increase the locational advantage of the depressed area relative to other, more prosperous areas of the economy. This should bring a substantial influx of new capital and thus greatly reduce the unemployment rate in the depressed area. This consideration suggests that the major depressed areas in the eastern United States are suitable candidates for capital subsidies to firms, for they are geographically near the major eastern markets. With some additional aid in developing overhead capital these areas could respond favorably to a capital subsidy. This consideration also implies that policy toward other depressed areas in the United States, particularly those isolated areas in the Mountain states, should be based more on training or wage subsidies than on capital subsidies. Such an emphasis should lead to a more efficient allocation of funds for regional subsidies and thus to an overall improvement in the status of all depressed areas in the economy.

In Canada, the likely success of some capital subsidies is not so great as in the United States. The major depressed areas, the Northwest and the Atlantic provinces, are on the perimeter of a large country and thus far removed from the major sources of domestic product demand. Instead, if politics prevent the use of migration subsidies in these areas, Canada should rely more heavily on subsidies aimed directly at increasing employment. If capital subsidies must be used, they should be restricted to social overhead capital and capital for export industries.

Another important factor to be considered is what effect increasing the capital stock of firms in the depressed area has on the productivity of labor. In particular, if this effect is relatively large, firms in the area will respond to capital subsidies by substantially increasing their employment. In such a case, the effect of the capital subsidy is to produce a large upward shift in the marginal productivity of labor. Given a constant wage rate in the area, the profit-maximizing firm will hire many more workers than it had previously employed.

In deciding upon which areas are likely to be good candidates for capital subsidies, planners should consider the magnitude of the cross-partial derivative of labor and capital in the production function. A higher value for it implies that subsidies for capital will be more successful in increasing employment. It can be related to measured quantities because it varies inversely with the elasticity of substitution between capital and labor.[13] If labor and capital are perfect substitutes, i.e., if the elasticity of substitution is infinite, this term is zero. In such a case, increasing capital has no effect whatsoever on the productivity of labor. On the other hand, as the elasticity of substitution approaches zero, slight increases in the capital stock of the firm produce very large increases in the firm's demand for labor. The government should seek to subsidize investment in those firms and industries in which the elasticity of substitution between capital and labor is relatively low.

There is substantial disagreement among economists about the empirical magnitudes of the elasticity of substitution in different industries. The best evidence suggests that on the whole these values do not differ very much from unity. There is evidence, albeit not very conclusive, that the elasticity of substitution in manufacturing is lower in durable goods industries than in nondurable goods; weak evidence in this direction has been produced in several studies using cross-section data.[14] It suggests that, in general, capital subsidies in depressed areas should be concentrated among firms in durable goods industries. In order to maintain equity with other firms, these latter should be offered subsidies for increasing employment directly. Such a flexible policy would lead to the most efficient use of subsidy funds while still maintaining neutrality among different industries and firms in the area.

In many areas, the success of a capital subsidy will hinge on the existence of adequate social overhead capital, particularly an adequate transportation system. The costs of this social investment must be added to the costs of the capital subsidies in comparing the program to alternatives aimed directly at increasing employment. Improving transportation between a depressed area and major consumer markets is likely to be cheapest, *ceteris paribus*, when the area is located near those markets. It seems likely, therefore, that there is a complementarity between the use of capital subsidies to firms and overhead capital subsidies.

Conclusions About Area Subsidies

Once society has decided upon how much it is willing to spend in helping depressed areas, it should next attempt to define whether its goal is increasing employment or increasing the amount of training embodied in workers in the area. As the two foregoing discussions showed, each of these goals implies that alternative strategies for subsidization in the area should be undertaken. If the goal is that of increasing employment, the major efforts should be aimed at subsidizing the training of workers using lump-sum grants. Under certain conditions of production, a capital subsidy to firms coupled with the development of social overhead capital might also be desirable in achieving this goal. If increasing the level of training is desired, the government should grant training funds to those firms exhibiting low turnover rates.

Our results demonstrate that subsidy policy should be tailored to the location of the area relative to other, more prosperous, labor markets in the country. It should also take into account the nature of production in the area, including such factors as the labor intensity of production and the substitutability between labor and capital. The generality of training offered by firms in the area must also be considered in deciding between alternative types of labor subsidies. Whether the goal involves increasing only employment, increasing only the level of training, or some combination of both, regional policy must be flexible enough to offer different subsidies depending upon the characteristics of the area being subsidized.

4

Shifting the Phillips Curve Through Manpower Training

In this chapter, we discuss the problem of improving the trade-off between unemployment and inflation, a trade-off commonly known as the Phillips curve. One of the possible effects of manpower training is that it can change the structure of the economy to allow macroeconomic policy to achieve lower rates of unemployment while holding inflation within an acceptable range. To the extent that society desires such a structural change, it is the economist's job to discover efficient means of effecting it and to analyze its likely consequences for other aspects of economic activity.

Training and the Phillips Curve

We shall take as given the assumption that the inflation-unemployment relationship exists in the short run, and we shall not be concerned with the possibility that it is not valid in the long run. This latter possibility, which has been discussed increasingly in the economics literature in the past few years, should not affect the efficacy or importance of manpower training in achieving what must be a short-run goal. Indeed, the short-run Phillips curve is consistent with the existence of a "normal" rate of unemployment and with the concomitant vertical long-run Phillips curve proposed by Friedman and others.[1] Our results should be of value no matter what view one takes about the possibility of picking a combination of inflation and unemployment and maintaining that combination indefinitely.

In the models to be discussed, we assume that the short-run trade-off results because of bottlenecks in production in different sectors of the labor market. Although this explanation of a short-run Phillips curve has not been discussed in conjunction with the long-run expectations arguments, the two are mutually consistent. One example of the bottleneck model in operation is that product demand in the machine tool sector may be such that there is no available supply of tool and die makers; simultaneously, there may be an excess supply of workers in the construction sector. We would then observe rising wages in the tool and die sector and, if wages are rigid downward, stable wages in the construction sector. In the aggregate, then, wages would be rising although there would exist some unemployment. In the long run, this problem would right itself as laborers accept training in the tool and die industry. In the short run, the supply to each industry is not perfectly elastic, and we might postulate following the model of Lipsey that this short-run inelasticity of supply is the factor underlying the existence of a short-run Phillips curve.[2]

Manpower training may be viewed as a way in which the short-run elasticities of supply of labor to each industry are increased. Such training increases the rapidity with which an unemployed worker is employed by firms in an industry experiencing an increased demand for labor. By providing training in occupations that are important in a particular industry the government decreases the labor costs faced by firms in that industry. Training thus mitigates to some extent the problem of simultaneous shortages of trained labor and surpluses of unskilled new entrants into the labor force.

We shall construct a model of the labor market which produces a Phillips curve similar to some of those which have been estimated for the United States in the post-war period. We focus attention on the assumptions needed to produce this result and discuss the extent to which they are realistic. Within the framework of this model we can analyze the appropriate allocation of training funds among different industries according to the objective characteristics of these industries. We shall thus be able to provide some detailed policy implications for spending a fixed budget on manpower training.

Although it is impossible to provide a realistic estimate of the total cost of producing some given shift in the short-run Phillips curve, we shall try to provide a minimum estimate of that cost in this chapter. It can be used to compare existing budgets to the probable requirements for producing a significant shift in the trade-off. It is also important to know whether funds should be provided for upgrading or for training for low-level jobs, given that a purpose of manpower training is that of shifting the Phillips curve. This problem is also discussed within the framework of an informal model containing several classes of labor, the demand for each of which varies over the business cycle.

Statement of the Goal and Its Acceptance

Although the United States economy was operating at a fairly high level of unemployment in the early 1960s, economic planners recognized the importance of manpower training in removing bottlenecks at the lower unemployment rates they hoped would prevail in the near future. Training programs were introduced partly as measures designed to prevent inflation as the economy reached full employment: "New federal programs of retraining and other measures to increase the adaptability of the labor force have been introduced. These improvements in the adaptability of the labor force to changing demand conditions should permit relatively low levels of unemployment to be achieved before bottlenecks become serious."[3]

Economists to the contrary, this goal did not receive the same acceptance by Congress or by the popular press as did the other goals already discussed. It was not mentioned during the debates leading up to the enactment of the MDTA in 1961 and 1962, nor was it discussed in any of the early studies of either the ARA or the MDTA conducted under the auspices of the Department of Labor.

In more recent years, there has been a broader realization of the importance of this goal as one justification of and use for manpower training. The financial press has cited the discussions of economists on this subject: "Professor Samuelson says that conceivably the Phillips curve could be altered by...encouraging structural changes in the economy and by stepping up the training of the labor force."[4] Training has also been espoused by public officials as a way of circumventing the dilemma of reducing the rate of inflation while not increasing the level of unemployment. Training has, indeed, become the main crutch on which some political arguments rest: "In our leveling-off process we intend to do everything we can to resist increases in unemployment and to help workers in new jobs."[5] Whether this crutch could ever provide adequate support can be doubted by neutral observers; it is difficult to believe that deflationary policies will succeed in producing increased demand for labor in one sector while reducing aggregate demand. Rather, it is more likely that a general deflationary policy would reduce labor demand in all sectors thus decreasing the value of training designed to place workers in new jobs.

During the ten years in which government-sponsored manpower training has existed in this country, the goal of shifting the trade-off between unemployment and inflation has been quite secondary. Planners have apparently not realized that this goal could be pursued in conjunction with any of the other goals or even that such a relationship might exist. The main use of this goal has been as a political palliative, first to remove fears of inflation as the economy approached full employment, and then to remove fears of increasing unemployment as the economy was deflated.

Previous Economic Discussions of This Goal

Although economists clearly recognize that manpower training can ameliorate the trade-off between inflation and unemployment, actual economic work in this area has been very slight. Peirce took the simple two-sector model constructed by Lipsey and discussed the effects of manpower training in this context.[6] He then discussed how such training can remove bottlenecks by increasing the short-run elasticity of labor supply to an industry experiencing a shortage.

Holt constructs a Phillips curve based on search behavior and upon the mismatching of job vacancies and unemployed workers.[7] In his model, the short-run Phillips curve arises because workers fail to lower their reservation wages enough to encourage them to search through firms in which vacancies exist.[8] In Holt's view, manpower policy, of which training programs are one component, can shift the curve by providing increased information about job opportunities to workers and about the availability of labor to firms. This increased information will lead to a more efficient search by both workers and firms and to a better matching of existing job vacancies with unemployed workers.

These two studies are the only economic work available in this area, and unfortunately they do not provide much more guide for policy than could be derived from simple observation using common sense. There are no implications about where training funds should be spent to shift the curve, nor is there any consideration of how much money such a shift would require. Both studies simply say that training programs will be efficacious in shifting the curve and demonstrate the mechanisms by which their effects occur.

Even these conclusions are not necessarily complete. If one uses an alternative model of the short-run Phillips curve, it is clear that increasing information may have detrimental effects as well. Consider a model in which the demand for a firm's product is given and the firm decides upon its labor inputs based upon its expectations about product demand. Substantial previous work has demonstrated that there exists a lag in the adjustment of labor input to demand for the product of a firm or industry, and this lag has been linked to the nature of hiring and layoff costs which face the firm.[9] In particular, Holt himself has postulated a total hiring-cost function of the form

$$H(t) = \delta' + \delta'' \left\{ \frac{\dot{E}(t)}{E(t)} \right\}^2 \tag{4.1}$$

where E is employment, $\dot{E}$ is the change in employment, δ' and δ'' are parameters and t is an index denoting time. It pays the profit-maximizing firm to spread its adjustment in employment over a number of periods so that it avoids incurring the substantial average hiring costs of expanding rapidly in one period. This spreading out of initial costs produces the observed lag.

Reasons for the quadratic shape of the total hiring-cost function are the lack of information about job availability on the part of unemployed workers and the lower quality of workers available as employment expands. These difficulties make it increasingly costly for a firm to try to expand employment rapidly, for the firm must engage in substantial recruitment and training expenditures. Government expenditures which increase the information available to workers should have the effect of decreasing the parameter δ'', i.e., of making the hiring-cost function less quadratic.

Since the effect of the government training and information program is to flatten out the hiring-cost function, we should expect that such a program would reduce the average lag of employment behind output. This reduction in the lag implies that while the short-run Phillips curve will be shifted, the rate of unemployment would vary more over the business cycle. This result occurs because, under the subsidy program, employers will maintain a more constant output per man and be less hesitant about varying their work force.

In terms of Figure 4–1, we can postulate an inverse short-run relationship

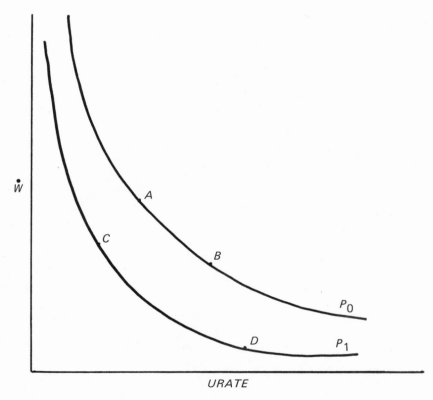

Figure 4–1. The Short-Run Phillips Curve and the Effects of Job-Matching Programs.

between the unemployment rate (URATE) and the rate of change of money wages. Assume current monetary and fiscal policies result in fluctuations on P_0 between points A and B. By increasing the amount of information in the labor market the government can change the structure of the economy and shift the curve to P_1 by ensuring a better match of jobs and workers. In doing so, however, it increases firms' willingness to vary employment, so that the same macroeconomic policies which before moved the economy between A and B now move it between C and D. Although wage inflation is generally less along P_1 than on P_0, unemployment at the cyclical trough is increased.

In conclusion, increasing information in one model does have the effect of shifting the Phillips curve. In another model, one which is at least as widely accepted, an additional important effect of such a subsidy program is to increase the volatility of employment in the economy. The desirability of such an increase depends very much on one's views about who benefits from various combinations of inflation and unemployment and upon whether wider fluctuations in employment lower expected rates of price increase and thus affect the future rate of inflation.

Industrial Characteristics and the Allocation of Training Funds in Shifting the Phillips Curve

In this section we present a multisector model of the labor market. The model hinges upon the numbers of workers having enough training to work in each sector. Because no data exist on these quantities, we use simulation techniques to analyze the model. Our model is designed to answer the question: How should a given amount of money be allocated among industries in order to produce the largest shift in the short-run relation between unemployment and the rate of inflation? The model is inspired by Lipsey's two-sector model, but it improves upon that early work in several ways: (1) Unlike the Lipsey model, it is explicitly dynamic.[10]. (2) It incorporates some assumptions about the labor market which are more consistent with the observed behavior of wages and employment.

In our model, we assume that the government training subsidy has the effect of increasing the short-run elasticity of labor supply to each industry. Additional training of unemployed new workers in occupations specific to an industry enables firms there to expand employment without encountering labor-market shortages. This is a far cheaper way of providing trained labor to expanding firms than would be a policy involving retraining of unemployed workers who already have been trained in occupations specific to other sectors. These latter workers are assumed to be rehired by their previous employers as output in other sectors expands.

We assume that there are four sectors in the economy, each with identical structural equations describing behavior in the sector. The parameters of these equations can be varied to simulate observable characteristics of different sectors in an actual economy. We use four sectors in order to achieve substantial variation in each of the parameters in which we are interested while still keeping the model small enough to permit a simple analysis of our results.

We further postulate that output demand is exogenous, that firms produce a fixed amount given by the exogenous incomes and tastes of consumers in the economy. The model is purely short run, so that capital stock is fixed throughout the simulation of the path of the economy. We ignore prices in our model and assume instead that productivity remains constant over the cycle, so that prices vary directly with wages. While this is a great simplification, it is one which enables us to concentrate on the main area in which manpower training has an effect, namely the removal of some of the bottlenecks in the labor market. To include a pricing sector in addition to the labor market would obfuscate the effects of manpower training and would digress from the discussion here. To the extent to which other changes in unit labor costs are more important than bottlenecks in the labor market in producing rises in prices, the results of our simulations must be qualified. Our assumptions about some of the parameters characterizing each of the sectors in our model are purely arbitrary because of a lack of available estimates of them. Other parameters do, on the average, correspond to observed characteristics in the real economy and can be taken to indicate the direction in which training funds should be allocated to achieve the goal of shifting the Phillips curve.

As we noted, output is exogenously determined by consumers' tastes and incomes. We assume further that there is a stable cycle in output, but one which is not symmetric over its duration. The initial output in each sector is the same; there is a trend in output over time; and we assume that the amplitude of the cycle in output varies among the sectors. The output for each sector is characterized by

$$
Y_i(t) = \begin{cases} YBAR_i(t)\left[1 + c_i \sin \dfrac{\pi Z}{16}\right] & \text{if } 0 \le Z \le 8 \\[2em] YBAR_i(t)\left[1 + c_i \sin \dfrac{\pi[Z-4]}{8}\right] & \text{if } Z > 8 \end{cases} \qquad i = 1,\dots,4 \quad (4.2)
$$

where c_i is the cyclicality parameter for output in the industry, $Y_i(t)$ is the industry's output, $YBAR_i(t)$ is the trend rate of output in the industry and $Z = t(\mathrm{mod}\ 20)$.[11] The detrended version of equation (4.2) generates a cycle similar to that depicted in Figure 4–2. Expansions are nearly twice the duration of contractions in this economy, an assumption that is not too unrealistic

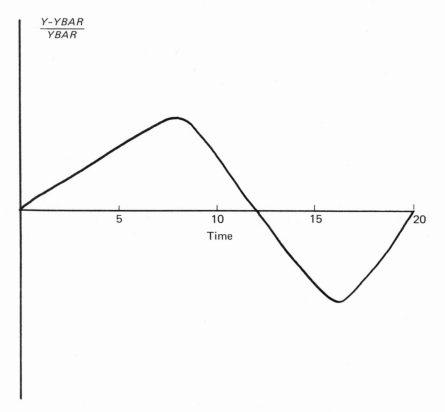

Figure 4–2. Time Path of Deviations of Output Around the Trend Value.

in the light of recent experience in the American economy.[12] Since our model is constructed with each time period equivalent to one quarter, the twenty-period cycle is also roughly consistent with experience in the post-war period up to the 1960s.

The model is assumed to be in dynamic equilibrium until time period zero, at which point output begins growing at different rates in each sector.

These trends in output are in addition to the cyclicality of output, and they are introduced into the model in order to capture the real-world phenomenon that the rate of growth of output in a sector is inversely related to its cyclicality of output. This fact is demonstrated by a comparison of the rankings of the parameters κ_1 and κ_2 based on the regressions

$$\log EQ_j(t) = \kappa_0 + \kappa_1 t + \kappa_2 \log U(t)$$

where j is the sector, EQ is its employment each month from 1948–1967, and U is the aggregate number of unemployed workers in the economy. As is shown in columns (1) and (2) of Table 4–1, this relationship is fairly clear; the rank correlation coefficient is -0.65, significant at the 5 percent level.

Table 4–1. Sector Growth, Cyclicality, and Unionization of Employment

Sector	(1) Growth[a]	(2) Cyclicality	(3) Unionization[b] (percent of production workers, 1960)
Mining	1	6	82
Construction	6	8	54
Durable manufacturing	4.5	10	}52
Nondurable manufacturing	2	7	
Transport, etc.	3	9	79
Wholesale trade	4.5	4	} 6
Retail trade	7	5	
Finance, etc.	8	1	2
Services	9	2	13
Public administration	10	3	14

[a] Lowest rank for slowest growth, least cyclical sectors.
[b] H. Gregg Lewis, *Unionism and Relative Wages in the United States* (Chicago: University of Chicago Press, 1963), p. 250.

We account for this relationship in our model by assuming an explicit relation between the parameter c_i and the rate of growth r_i included in

$$YBAR_i(t) = YBAR_i(0)[1 + r_i]^t \qquad i = 1, \ldots, 4$$

In particular, we assume that

$$r_i = \theta_0 + \theta_1 c_i \qquad \theta_1 < 0 \quad i = 1, \ldots, 4 \tag{4.3}$$

where θ_0 and θ_1 are fixed parameters to be chosen so that the average rate of growth in employment, $\bar{r}$, is 0.0025 per period or approximately 1 percent per year. This value is designed to reflect roughly the trend rate of growth in the United States labor force. Since we rule out technical change in this model the growth rates in output and employment can be assumed to be identical.

We assume that each firm in each of the sectors in the economy is a perfect competitor in the market for labor available to the industry. Furthermore, each firm in a specific sector is faced by identical supply curves and by an identical wage rate for labor which is homogeneous once it has been hired and trained in the industry. Production functions are also identical for all firms in an industry, and each production function is characterized by the distribution parameter $[1 - \alpha_i]$ for labor. Since we are ignoring prices in this model, we may assume that the price simply equals the wage in the industry, so that in our final marginal productivity condition describing the firm's equilibrium employment the price and wage terms drop out. This leaves us with

$$E_i^*(t) = \frac{[1 - \alpha_i] Y_i(t)}{H} \qquad i = 1, \ldots, 4 \qquad (4.4)$$

where E_i^* is equilibrium employment in the industry and H, hours worked, is assumed to be 40 throughout our simulations. This description of the optimizing employment in the firm could be derived equally well from a fixed-coefficients production function; and, given our assumption about wages and prices, this equation could be modified slightly to fit the entire class of CES production functions.

As we discussed earlier, it is commonly accepted in the literature that a lag exists between employment and output. Although it has been demonstrated that different lags in adjustment seem appropriate when the firm is increasing instead of decreasing employment, we nonetheless assume here that the lag is the same for both changes.[13] Since all of the components of hiring costs differ among industries, we may assume that the parameters λ_i characterizing this lag also differ in the several sectors of the economy. We use a simple adaptive-expectations model to characterize the rate at which firms adjust actual employment, E_i, to desired employment.[14] This simple assumption, which gives rise to a lag structure with geometrically declining weights, is reflected in

$$E_i(t) - E_i(t - 1) = \lambda_i[E_i^*(t) - E_i(t - 1)] \quad i = 1, \ldots, 4 \qquad (4.5)$$

These two sets of equations, (4.4) and (4.5), characterize the demand side of the labor market.

The novel part of our model is its description of the supply of labor to the several sectors. We assume that no bottleneck exists if employment demand in a sector is less than or equal to the highest previous employment in that sector. We thus assume that once workers have been employed in an industry they supply themselves to that industry at the existing wage rate. Bottlenecks arise when employment demand is such that there no longer exists a pool of unemployed labor which has already been trained for work in the particular sector. In such cases firms must raise wages to induce workers to accept training in the sector.

In performing the simulations, we assume that the actual supply constraint is not the highest past employment, but rather the highest past employment less some amount depending upon the point in time at which the past peak was reached. We incorporate this assumption in our economy to reflect the notion that there are exits from the labor force due to death or retirement. At any point in time, the total pool of trained labor available to an industry can be described by

$$EPOOL_i(t) = \frac{EPP_i(t)}{1.005^{q_i}} \qquad i = 1, ..., 4 \qquad (4.6)$$

where $EPOOL_i$ is the pool of trained labor; EPP_i is the highest past employment and q_i is the number of periods elapsed since the previous peak in employment in the industry. We thus assume that exits from the labor force occur at a rate of 0.5 percent per period or approximately 2 percent per year. This figure is a fairly close approximation to the actual exits occurring because of deaths and retirements.[15] In order to ensure an average growth rate of employment equal to $\bar{r}$ we assume that entry into the labor force occurs at the rate of 0.75 percent per period.

The supply of labor to the industry thus depends on the available pool of existing trained workers. We assume that wages in the industry relative to the wage level in the economy as a whole are a function of the ratio of this amount and the actual employment in the industry, and that relative wages adjust with a lag because of rigidities in the labor market. These assumptions produce the curves

$$\frac{W_i(t)}{WBAR(t-1)} = \left(\frac{E_i(t)}{EPOOL_i(t)}\right)^{\beta_i} \cdot \left(\frac{W_i(t-1)}{WBAR(t-2)}\right)^{\gamma_i} \qquad i = 1, ..., 4 \qquad (4.7)$$

where W_i is the wage in the industry and $WBAR$ is a weighted average of wages in the industries using as weights the employment in each industry. The parameter β_i is the inverse of the initial increase in wages in response to a rise in employment demand. The parameter γ_i measures the average duration of the lag in adjustment of wages to shortages in supply of labor to the industry; if γ_i is higher, the lag in relative wages is longer. Our formulation of this relationship and the assumptions made about the time path of output in each sector ensure that there is no long-run wage divergence in our results.

In order to add further realism to this model we postulate that the average lag in wages is inversely related to the cyclicality parameter. The more cyclical the output in an industry, the more rapidly supply adjusts to bring relative wages into equilibrium and the smaller the wage increase needed. There is no assumption of causality here; rather, we use cyclicality to indicate those sectors which are more heavily unionized. In industries in which unions exert some influence on relative wages, we should expect there to be a large number of untrained workers waiting to seek employment as labor demand increases. The high wages in these sectors ensure firms of a rapidly adjusting labor supply which draws on workers in sectors where wages are not maintained above competitive rates. By comparing columns (2) and (3) in Table 4–1 we see that the extent of unionism (and presumably its effect on average wages) is less in those sectors in which output is less cyclical. Indeed, the rank correlation between column (2) and the ranked version of column (3) is -0.72, easily significant at the 5 percent level. We can therefore postulate that

$$\gamma_i = 0.75 - g[c_i - c] \qquad i = 1, ..., 4 \qquad (4.8)$$

where g is a parameter which varies in our simulations and which indicates the strength of the relationship between γ_i and c_i. Equation (4.8) implies that the economy-wide rate of adjustment of labor supply is 0.75, i.e., that half of the supply adjustment is made in 2.5 quarters.

To complete this part of the model we make the following assumption about wages in each sector

$$W_i(t) \geq W_i(t - 1) \qquad i = 1, ..., 4 \qquad (4.9)$$

This assumption of wages which are rigid downward is discussed by the Webbs and is included in Keynes.[16] Whether due to union combination or simply to the refusal of each individual worker to accept a cut in wages, it appears to be quite consistent with observed behavior over the last few decades.[17]

In order to complete the model we need only to present equations linking employment in the individual sectors to the aggregate labor supply. Following substantial recent work in the area of the cyclical behavior of the labor force, we assume that the size of the total labor force depends both on the population and on the unemployment rate.[18] The particular equation we use is

$$L(t) = \left[-0.26\,\frac{U(t-1)}{L(t-1)} + 0.58 \right] POP(t) \qquad (4.10)$$

where U is the number of unemployed workers, L is the labor force, and POP is the population which is growing at the rate $\bar{r}$. The actual coefficient used to link the labor force to the unemployment rate is that derived from estimates based on the behavior of persons aged 14 years and over for the years 1954–1965 by Bowen and Finegan.[19] Although the use of cyclical variation in the labor force is not essential to the model, it does provide some additional realism with no extra computational or analytical expense.

As we discussed above, we assume that government subsidized manpower training affects the economy by increasing the short-run labor supply elasticity to the industry for which the training is provided. This assumption is embodied in equation (4.11)

$$\beta_i = \frac{1}{b_i + T_i/z} \qquad i = 1,...,4 \qquad (4.11)$$

where b_i is a parameter characterizing supply in this industry (if there is no subsidy it is simply the supply elasticity), z is a constant identical in all sectors, and T_i is the amount of money spent by the government on training for occupations in the particular sector.

The assumption of a constant training efficiency z, which is an indication of the costs of producing a trained worker in sector i, may not be correct. It is likely that training requirements are postively related to unionization, for it is easier for unions to restrict supply where skill requirements are greater. We should thus expect that unionization has occurred chiefly in those areas where high levels of training permit union labor to differentiate itself from potential substitutes. This correlation and the relation between unionization and the cyclicality of output suggest that z may be greater in more cyclical industries. To the extent that this is valid, our simulation results will provide an underestimate of the proportion of the training budget which should be spent on training for occupations in less cyclical industries.

There are several problems in interpreting our assumptions about the effects of training on the structure of the model. First of all, we must assume that there is no overlap of skills between sectors, that each occupation is specific to one industry. This assumption allows us to conclude that any money spent in training for a particular industry affects only the supply elasticity in that particular industry. There is no spillover into the other industries which might increase the supply elasticity in those industries. Second, we must assume for simplicity that training expenditures are identical in each sector throughout the whole period in which the path of the economy is simulated. We are not solving a dynamic programming problem concerning the allocation of training expenditures over time. Rather, we are inquiring into the steady-state distribution of money for training among different industries. Thus, whether training has a one-shot effect or a lifelong effect on the supply behavior of the workers trained, such differences have no bearing on the results of our model.

There are four parameters which take on different values in the four different sectors. These are: (1) $[1 - \alpha_i]$, the labor intensity of production; (2) λ_i, the lag in adjustment of employment to output; (3) b_i, the short-run elasticity of labor supply in the industry in which no subsidy is received; and (4) c_i, the cyclical variation in exogenous output. In addition, the parameter g will be varied in our simulations. These five parameters can be linked to values characterizing actual industries in the economy, and it is these parameters which will be varied in our discussion of how a fixed training budget can be allocated to achieve the maximum shift in the short-run Phillips curve.

Simulation Procedures and Results

In order to generate a stable path for the economy described by our model, it is necessary to find equilibrium solutions to the model. We compute these by setting the past values of the endogenous variables equal to their current period values. Table 4–2 presents the values of each parameter in each of the seven simulations. The values of the parameters POP_0 and $ETOT_0$ (the sum of initial equilibrium employment in the four sectors) were derived so that the simulations result in an average unemployment rate of approximately 4 percent during the cycle. Initial equilibrium output $YBAR_i(0)$ is assumed to be 250,000 units in each sector. The average values of each of the five varying parameters are taken to correspond as closely as possible to the values observed in empirical studies of the United States economy in the post-war period. The value 0.65 for the labor intensity of production corresponds quite closely to that provided in numerous estimates, the earliest of which was that of Douglas.[20] The parameter describing the lag in adjustment of employment to output is assumed to be 0.5, implying an average lag of one quarter.[21] This value is substantially less than that estimated in one early study but is in line with those values found in more recent work.

Table 4–2. Combinations of Parameters Used in the Simulations

		Simulation Number						
		1	2	3	4	5	6	7
Parameter varied in the simulation		$1-\alpha$	λ	b	c	c	c	c
Its value in sector	1	0.9000	0.2000	3.0000	0		same	
	2	0.8000	0.3333	2.0000	0.0200		as	
	3	0.5000	0.7500	0.7500	0.0400		simulation	
	4	0.4000	0.9375	0.3333	0.0600		4	
Other parameters (same value in each sector)								
$1-\alpha$			0.6500	0.6500	0.6500	0.6500	0.6500	0.6500
λ		0.5000		0.5000	0.5000	0.5000	0.5000	0.5000
b		1.0000	1.0000		1.0000	1.0000	1.0000	1.0000
c		0.0300	0.0300	0.0300				
γ		0.7500	0.7500	0.7500	0.7500			
g		3.0000	3.0000	3.0000	0.0000	2.0000	4.0000	6.0000
POP_0		29717	29717	29717	29717	29717	29717	29717
$YBAR_0$		250000	250000	250000	250000	250000	250000	250000
$ETOT_0$		16250[a]	16250	16250	16250	16250	16250	16250

[a] In simulation 1, $EI_0 = 5625, 5000, 3125$, and 2500 in sectors 1–4 respectively; in the other simulations $EI_0 = 4062.5$ in each sector.

$1 - \alpha =$ labor intensity of production.

λ characterizes the lag in adjustment of employment to output.

b = short-run labor supply elasticity.

c = cyclicality of production.

g = parameter describing the relation between c and the lag in the adjustment of relative wages.

The average value of c is 0.03, implying that the amplitude of fluctuations in output is 6 percent. Lags in employment adjustment and the discouraged-worker effect on labor force participation make fluctuations in unemployment less severe than those in output and cause them to correspond closely to those observed in the post-war period. (The average difference between peak and trough unemployment rates in the United States from 1948–1961 is 3.1 percentage points.[22]) Since the growth rates of employment in the large sectors listed in Table 4–1 range from -0.5 to 1 percent per quarter, and since we wish to link the values of the parameters c_i to r_i using equation (4.3), we assume that $\theta_0 = 0.01$ and $\theta_1 = -0.25$.

In the case of the short-run supply elasticity and the lag in adjustment of relative wages there is no obvious correspondence between our assumptions about these parameters and their real-world values. There have been no really satisfactory estimates of these parameters, so that our assumptions about them are purely arbitrary.

Each of the five simulations is performed on the economy in which no training program is provided by the government. The model is allowed to run for 100 periods so that it should converge to some stable cyclical pattern. During the first 60 periods we assume $r_i = 0$ for all sectors, to allow the economy to generate its own dynamic equilibrium path. The last 20 periods of each simulation run are then used to estimate the short-run Phillips curve characterizing the economy in which no training program is present. This curve is then compared to the curves generated by each of a large number of different allocations of the total training budget. We assume that the total training budget is exactly 1 percent of total output in the economy. The budget is divided into tenths and Phillips curves characterizing all possible allocations of these portions are computed. The most efficient solution is that which generates a curve for which the shift, as compared to the curve produced in the unsubsidized case, is at a maximum. In the second round, this efficient solution is taken and the budget is divided into fiftieths. We then search in the neighborhood of the first-round solution using this new grid for that allocation which maximizes the shift in the curve.

On first glance it appears that there are an infinite number of ways of computing the magnitude of the shift in the curve. One might, for example, take the integral of the difference between the two curves; one might weight the values of the shift at the lower unemployment rates more highly; or one might weight more highly the values at higher unemployment rates. Each of these weighting schemes corresponds to some implicit social utility function indicated by the policy makers concerned. In fact, this problem is of slight importance in our model because of the way in which the Phillips curve is estimated and because of our assumption of downward wage-rate rigidity. We estimate a curve of the sort

$$\dot{W} = a' + a'' URATE^{-1}$$

where $\dot{W}$ is the quarterly percentage change in $WBAR$ and $URATE$ is U/L. Since the value of $\dot{W}$ is never negative, the parameter a' is approximately zero. Thus, in our simulations the most efficient solutions are identical whether we weight the shift more heavily at the higher end or at the lower end of the unemployment scale.

Before we discuss how the optimal allocations of the training budget vary with changes in the industrial characteristics, it is worth noting how closely the simulation results approximate observed behavior of unemployment and wages. The peak-to-trough change in the unemployment rate ranges from 3.25 to 3.7 percentage points, roughly equal to the post-war average. The regression coefficients in the wage–unemployment equations range from 5 to 20. In an equation covering manufacturing from 1948–1961, we derived the estimate of 23 for this coefficient based on quarterly data *using annual rates of change in wages.*[23] This figure is within the range of our simulation estimates when these latter are adjusted to account for our use of quarter-to-quarter rates of change. It is very reassuring that the use of estimates of structural parameters derived from a number of different sources produces observations on macroeconomic variables whose relationships are similar to those between real-world observations on the same variables.

In Table 4–3 we present the allocations of the training budget which

Table 4–3. Simulation Results for Variations in Labor Intensity, Employment Lags, and Short-Run Supply Elasticities

	Sector			
	1	2	3	4
Parameter $1 - \alpha =$	0.90	0.800	0.50	0.400
Percent of training subsidy	48	40	12	0
Value of subsidized b	1.48	1.40	1.12	1.00
Range of *URATE*		(2.26, 5.93)		
Unsubsidized regression equation		$\dot{W} = -0.0094 + 9.79 URATE^{-1}$		
Subsidized regression equation		$\dot{W} = -0.0073 + 7.61 URATE^{-1}$		
Parameter $\lambda =$	0.20	0.3333	0.75	0.9375
Average lag (in quarters)	3.11	1.71	0.50	0.25
Percentage of training subsidy	22	26	26	26
Value of subsidized b	1.22	1.26	1.26	1.26
Range of *URATE*		(2.51, 5.76)		
Unsubsidized regression equation		$\dot{W} = -0.0092 + 10.11 URATE^{-1}$		
Subsidized regression equation		$\dot{W} = -0.0074 + 8.06 URATE^{-1}$		
Parameter $b =$	3.00	2.0000	0.75	0.3333
Percentage of training subsidy	0	0	30	70
Value of susidized b	1.00	1.00	1.30	1.70
Range of *URATE*		(2.26, 5.93)		
Unsubsidized regression equation		$\dot{W} = -0.0119 + 13.09 URATE^{-1}$		
Subsidized regression equation		$\dot{W} = -0.0064 + 6.73 URATE^{-1}$		

produce the maximum shift in the simple relationship between aggregate wage-rate changes and the rate of unemployment. For each of the simulations in which $[1 - \alpha]$, λ, and b vary we list the value of the short-run supply elasticity which occurs under the efficient allocation of training funds. This is done in order to allow comparisons between the values of the varying parameters and the manner in which the maximizing shift is produced. In addition, we present the equations for the unsubsidized curve and for the maximizing, subsidized curve for each of the seven simulations. We include only the simple bivariate relationship between wage changes and the unemployment rate in order to make presentation of the results easier. This is not strictly correct, for when the unemployment rate is dropping the wage change is somewhat higher than is predicted by the unemployment rate alone. To be correct, we should have introduced a term for the rate of change in the unemployment rate. We did not do this because many empirical studies of the trade-off in the United States fail to find that this second variable is significant. In any case, the bivariate regressions usually explain 90 percent of the variance in $\dot{W}$. The unemployment rate itself is included in inverse form to correspond with the results of a number of econometric studies of the Phillips curve in the United States.[24]

In the case of the labor intensity parameter, $[1 - \alpha]$, the money should be spent more heavily in those sectors in which production is more labor intensive. Money is spent in sector 1, which has a labor intensity slightly less than twice that of sector 3, to produce an increase in the supply elasticity which is four times as great as that produced in sector 3. Apparently, there is a more than proportionate payoff to concentrating money in those sectors which are highly labor intensive.

As we discussed previously, models can be built in which information has the effect of increasing the variation in the number of employed workers over the cycle. This result depended upon information affecting the speed with which firms adjust employment to meet changes in expected product demand. Our results here show that, in a model which produces a reasonable short-run Phillips curve, the rate at which the adjustment takes place has no effect on the optimizing allocation of training funds. The slight differences in the allocation across the four sectors are due to our method of searching, for an equal allocation of money into identical quarters in a sector was not possible because of the grid over which we searched.

The results on the short-run supply elasticity are especially interesting. The efficient allocation of the fixed budget for training results in no money spent in either of the two sectors in which the supply elasticity is relatively large. Rather, all the money is spent in those two sectors which have relatively low supply elasticities. This result suggests the importance of concentrating money in so-called bottleneck sectors of the economy. By assumption, such a sector in our model is one in which the supply elasticity is low. It is really quite surprising that, despite the spillovers embodied in our model, the efficient solution still suggests that all of the funds be concentrated in these sectors.

In Table 4–4, we list the results of the simulations under the assumption

Table 4–4. Simulation Results for Variations in the Cyclicality of Production and the Relation to Lags in the Adjustment of Wages

	Sector			
	1	2	3	4
Parameters $c =$	0	0.02	0.0400	0.06
$\gamma =$	0.75	0.75	0.75	0.75
Average lag (in quarters)	2.41	2.41	2.41	2.41
Percent of training subsidy	60	36	4	0
Value of subsidized b	1.60	1.36	1.04	1.00
Range of $URATE$		(2.53, 5.73)		
Unsubsidized regression equation		$\dot{W} = -0.0082 + 5.32 URATE^{-1}$		
Subsidized regression equation		$\dot{W} = -0.0059 + 3.47 URATE^{-1}$		
Parameters $c =$	0	0.02	0.0400	0.0600
$\gamma =$	0.81	0.77	0.73	0.69
Average lag (in quarters)	3.29	2.65	2.20	1.87
Percent of training subsidy	70	30	0	0
Value of subsidized b	1.70	1.30	1.00	1.00
Range of $URATE$		(2.53, 5.73)		
Unsubsidized regression equation		$\dot{W} = -0.0103 + 7.20 URATE^{-1}$		
Subsidized regression equation		$\dot{W} = -0.0077 + 4.50 URATE^{-1}$		
Parameters $c =$	0	0.02	0.04	0.06
$\gamma =$	0.87	0.79	0.71	0.63
Average lag (in quarters)	4.98	2.94	2.02	1.50
Percent of training subsidy	82	18	0	0
Value of subsidized b	1.82	1.18	1.00	1.00
Range of $URATE$		(2.53, 5.73)		
Unsubsidized regression equation		$\dot{W} = -0.0122 + 10.70 URATE^{-1}$		
Subsidized regression equation		$\dot{W} = -0.0100 + 6.20 URATE^{-1}$		
Parameters $c =$	0	0.02	0.04	0.06
$\gamma =$	0.93	0.81	0.69	0.57
Average lag (in quarters)	9.56	3.29	1.87	1.23
Percent of training subsidy	100	0	0	0
Value of subsidized b	2.00	1.00	1.00	1.00
Range of $URATE$		(2.53, 5.73)		
Unsubsidized regression equation		$\dot{W} = -0.0023 + 21.03 URATE^{-1}$		
Subsidized regression equation		$\dot{W} = -0.0012 + 10.17 URATE^{-1}$		

that the cyclicality parameters vary across industries. In the first of these simulations, when the lags in supply adjustment of labor are identical in each industry, we find that the majority of the training subsidy is spent in the least cyclical sector while none of the money is spent in that sector in which the output is most strongly cyclical. This conclusion results from our inclusion of the relationship in equation (4.3) between cyclicality and the trend rate of output growth. While some bottlenecks do arise in those sectors in which output has the highest cyclical variation, the major bottlenecks are caused by steady expansion in output in the least cyclical industries.

Not surprisingly, as the relation between c_i and γ_i becomes stronger, we find that the percentage of the training subsidy allocated to the least cyclical sector increases. When the parameter g is larger, the lag in the adjustment of labor supply in the least cyclical sector is relatively greater than the comparable lag in the most cyclical sector. Since lags in supply adjustment perpetuate the inflationary pressures exerted by initial inelasticities in supply, those sectors in which the lags are greater will be ones where the training subsidy should be applied most heavily. Indeed, when we assume a very strong relation between c_i and γ_i, as in the final simulation in Table 4–4, we find that the entire training subsidy is allocated to the least cyclical sector where the supply lag is longest.

The precise details in the allocation of training money across the several sectors should not be taken very seriously. Serious consideration should be given, however, to the notion that in a labor-market model that produces reasonable results we can identify certain factors which should be guiding the allocation of training funds. Labor intensity of production; the degree of cyclical variation and trend in product demand; and factors which are harder to isolate, namely the short-run elasticities of labor supply and the lags in adjustment of relative wages, all should be considered in deciding in which occupations and industries funds should be spent for training.

Empirical Correlates of Selected Simulation Parameters

As we noted above, a number of objective characteristics of the economy can be used by manpower planners who wish to be efficient in achieving the goal of shifting the short-run trade-off between inflation and unemployment. For that reason, then, we will relate some of the parameters used in our simulations to estimates of their values in a number of the industries in the United States economy.

Manufacturing, mining, transportation, and construction are among the more cyclical industries in the economy; and our results suggest that, because of the relationship between cyclicality and growth in output, training funds should be allocated to sectors other than these. Additional force for this argument is provided when we recognize that these sectors probably require greater than average training expenditures per man. The labor intensity of production is also important in determining the allocation of training funds. In Chapter 2 we discussed this parameter and made the argument that production in manufacturing and certain service industries is more labor-intensive than production in the economy as a whole. For this reason, we may conclude that our model implies on this basis as well that money should be concentrated in the service sector, other things equal.

We demonstrated above that variations in the parameter λ have no effect on the allocation of training funds if we assume that these funds have their influence through the supply elasticity. If, however, training money also affects the lag in adjustment of employment to output by changing the amount of information available to workers and firms, we should consider variations in this parameter. In particular, if the government wishes to achieve wider fluctuations in employment over the business cycle, it should concentrate training money in those sectors in which the lag in adjustment of employment to output is relatively long. If, on the other hand, it has the opposite goal, the government should concentrate its money in sectors in which the rate of adjustment is already rather rapid.

Table 4–5 presents lags in hiring and laying off of manufacturing workers estimated from monthly data for the period 1958–1966. A high value in the first column indicates a long lag in hiring, and a high value in the second column indicates that the lag in laying off is long. Because these parameters were computed using monthly rather than quarterly data, one must transform them to make them exactly comparable to the parameters used in the simulations. One transformation is

$$\lambda_s = 1 - (1 - \lambda_i)^3$$

where λ_s is a parameter used in the simulations and $(1 - \lambda_i)$ is any estimated parameter listed in Table 4–5. With the exception of the two small industries in the larger group called chemicals, we can conclude from this table that the lags are greater in the durable goods industries than in nondurable manufacturing. We might infer from this that the hiring cost functions for these durable goods industries have a quadratic term which is more important than that in their counterparts for the nondurable goods industries. If policy makers desire wider fluctuations in employment over the business cycle, money should be concentrated in durable manufacturing. If, on the other hand, this is not a goal of policy, information should be disseminated more among nondurable goods industries and any other industries in which initial costs lead to relatively short lags in adjustment of employment.

It is extremely difficult to derive empirical estimates of the supply elasticities of labor to particular industries. Presumably the supply elasticity is less and the lags in adjustment are longer for those industries in which more training specific to the industry is required. *Ceteris paribus*, bottlenecks are more likely to arise in these industries because of the need for larger investments in training workers who seek to enter them in response to increases in labor demand. Unfortunately, training requirements are so highly correlated

Table 4–5. Lags in Hiring and Laying off in Selected Industries

SIC	Industry	$(1 - \lambda_1)$	$(1 - \lambda_2)$
336	Nonferrous foundries	.873	.633
263	Paperboard	.573	.335
301	Tires and inner tubes	.819	.644
242	Sawmills and planing mills	.820	.844
2431	Millwork	.730	.722
2432	Veneer and plywood	.674	.815
3221	Glass containers	.118	0
324	Cement, hydraulic	.708	.578
3251	Brick and structural clay tile	.679	.712
332	Iron and steel foundries	.939	.875
3352	Aluminum rolling, drawing and extruding	.728	.720
341	Metal cans	.499	.217
3433	Heating equipment	.759	.631
3632	Household refrigerators and freezers	.789	.606
3633	Household laundry equipment	.496	.722
365	Radio and TV receiving sets	.777	.678
207	Confectionary and related products	.592	.332
211	Cigarettes	.780	.580
212	Cigars	.651	.655
223	Wool weaving and finishing	.812	.765
231	Men's and boys' suits and coats	.817	.731
232	Men's and boys' furnishings	.825	.731
2653	Corrugated and solid fiber boxes	0	0
2821	Plastic materials and resins	.898	.030
2823, 4	Synthetic fibers	.771	.838
302, 3, 6	Other rubber products	.702	.661
311	Leather tanning and finishing	.675	0
314	Footwear, except rubber	.805	.560

Source: Daniel Hamermesh, "A Disaggregative Econometric Model of Gross Changes in Employment," *Yale Economic Essays*, 9 (Fall 1969): 122.

with the extent of unionization (which, we argued, is negatively correlated with lags in supply adjustment), that it is impossible to guess the direction of the relation between training and lags in supply.

Upgrading vs. Entry-Level Training

In the previous sections of this chapter, we have operated within the framework of a group of industries, each of which contains only one occupation. In this section, we discuss the allocation of training funds among occupations within a particular industry. An important debate exists among manpower experts about whether money should be spent on training for entry-level jobs or on upgrading workers who are already employed. A choice between these two alternatives has significant implications for an antipoverty policy, but since the central goal being discussed in this chapter is that of improving the trade-off between inflation and unemployment, we consider the effects of various strategies on this particular goal alone.

We can construct a typology of three alternative strategies available to the government: (1) T_{01}, training of unemployed workers for entry-level jobs, (2) T_{12}, training of entry-level employees for jobs requiring more skills, (3) T_{02}, training of unemployed workers for higher-level and more skilled jobs. The question to be asked is: What combination of these three strategies should be pursued, and under what conditions should that combination be varied?

It seems fairly clear that the strategy T_{02} is inconsistent with the goal of efficient use of manpower training to shift the short-run Phillips curve. We can assume that the costs of training a worker who is already employed at an entry-level job for a higher-skilled one must be less than the costs of training an unemployed, unskilled worker for such a higher-level job. Since the goal of such training is to remove bottlenecks in higher-skilled employment, the same number of trained, higher-skilled workers can be supplied for less money by training current entry-level employees. The aim of shifting the Phillips curve efficiently requires that unemployed workers be trained only for entry-level jobs.

In deciding what mix of strategies T_{01} and T_{12} to pursue, we assume that the shortages for occupations 2, higher-skilled occupations, are greater than those for occupations 1, the entry-level occupations. This assumption is supported by the data on unemployment rates by occupation presented in Table 4–6 for both cyclical troughs and peaks. Moreover, as is demonstrated by the data in Table 4–7, the same phenomenon appears to exist in a number of countries. (The nations selected are those for which comparable data are available.) Professional and white-collar occupations generally exhibit lower rates of unemployment than do blue-collar occupations.

Two cases must be considered. If there is no shortage of occupation 1, but there is some excess demand for occupation 2, the government should finance only strategy T_{12}, the upgrading strategy. The upgrading of entry-level workers should have the additional value of providing entry-level openings for job applicants for whom no openings previously existed. Thus, this strategy has the important indirect effect of alleviating unemployment among unskilled workers in addition to its direct effect of removing shortages in skilled occupations.[25] If shortages exist for both occupations, a mix of

Table 4–6. Seasonally Adjusted Unemployment Rates by Occupation Group for Recent Cyclical Troughs and Peaks

	Trough April 1958	Peak May 1960	Trough February 1961	Peak[a] July 1969	Trough[a] December 1970
Professional and technical	2.0	1.5	2.1	1.4	2.9
Managers, officials, etc.	1.9	1.4	2.0	0.8	1.7
Clerical	5.0	3.6	4.6	3.1	5.3
Sales	4.4	3.9	4.6	3.2	5.1
Craftsman and foremen	7.3	4.4	6.8	1.9	5.0
Operatives	12.9	7.6	10.8	4.2	9.0
Nonfarm laborers	16.6	11.1	14.1	7.0	11.0
Service	7.3	5.6	7.2	4.3	6.2
Aggregate	7.4	5.1	6.9	3.5	6.2

[a] Estimated date of cyclical peak or trough.
Source: Employment and Earnings (February 1971), pp. 184–185.

Table 4–7. Unemployment Rates by Occupation Group in Selected Countries

Year Survey Taken	Canada 1961	Korea 1968	Syria 1967	Spain 1968	Greece 1961	Sweden 1965
Professional and technical	2.5	2.7	1.0	0.3	0.9	0.7
Managers, officials, etc.		8.5	0.6	0.2	0.2	
Clerical		3.8	1.2	0.5	2.9	0.9
Sales		3.1	2.2	0.3	0.9	1.0
Transport and communications	9.3	5.9	5.5	1.0	1.9	0.9
Craftsmen, operatives and laborers not elsewhere classified	11.0	5.0	9.3	1.9	8.0	1.5
Service	6.0	2.8	3.1	0.7	2.4	1.8

Source: Computed from International Labor Office, *Yearbook of Labor Statistics,* 1969, pp. 42–261, 396–433.

strategies T_{01} and T_{12} seems desirable. Even in this latter case, however, our assumption of greater shortages in occupation 2 requires that the bulk of the training expenditures be concentrated in this latter occupation. In any event, the mix clearly depends on the aggregate level of activity. As the aggregate rate of unemployment increases, the data in Table 4–6 suggest that shortages of workers for entry-level jobs cease to exist and only shortages for higher-skilled jobs remain. Thus, as an economy retreats from a cyclical peak, training money should be concentrated more on training for higher-skilled employment.

The actual mix of strategies T_{01} and T_{12} in a time of low aggregate unemployment depends on several factors which are very difficult to estimate empirically. The relative costs of each type of training which would be incurred by the government must be known before a determination of the optimal mix can be made. Furthermore, the propensities of firms to train one type of labor if the other is subsidized must also be known. This latter factor depends upon the elasticities of substitution between the different skills as well as on the elasticities of supply of these skills to the different industries. In addition, customary practices of promotion along different "job ladders" must also be considered.[26] All of these factors are extremely difficult to isolate, and no definitive discussions of them have yet been offered.

Tables 4–8 and 4–9 present the available information on the distribution of trainees by occupation during the lifetime of the MDTA. It appears from these data that institutional training has become increasingly concentrated in professional and clerical occupations since the inception of this program. These occupations account for much greater proportions of institutional training than they do of on-the-job training. The JOBS program also has only a tiny percentage of its total enrollment in the professional occupations.

Table 4–8. Occupational Distribution of MDTA Institutional Trainees, 1963–1966

| Occupation Group | Calendar Year | | | |
	1963	1964	1965	1966
Professional, technical, and managerial	10.0	9.6	8.5	9.8
Clerical and sales	21.4	22.5	21.6	16.3
Service	9.8	13.1	13.2	16.3
Agriculture	2.5	4.3	3.6	4.2
Skilled occupations	31.7	28.4	25.5	19.6
Semiskilled occupations	22.2	16.8	17.0	18.2
Other	2.5	5.3	10.6	15.5

Note: Percents may not add to 100 due to rounding.
Source: Education and Training, 1967, p. 85, report of the Secretary of Health, Education and Welfare to Congress on the MDTA.

Table 4–9. Occupational Distributions of MDTA Institutional and On-the-Job Trainees and of JOBS Enrollees, 1967–1970

Occupation	Institutional		OJT		JOBS
	FY67	FY68	FY67	FY68	Feb. 1970
Professional, technical, and managerial	12.4	15.2	3.3	3.1	3.8
Clerical and sales	20.4	20.3	8.7	9.2	24.5
Service	17.0	15.0	15.1	16.3	5.5
Farming, fishery, and forestry	2.3	1.4	1.2	0.3	0.5
Processing	1.1	0.5	0.6	1.3	11.0
Machine trades	21.3	22.4	27.7	22.3	12.0
Bench work	6.2	5.2	15.0	13.3	11.7
Structural work	17.7	18.3	16.9	21.1	15.5
Miscellaneous and unknown	1.6	1.7	11.5	13.1	15.5

Source: (1)–(4): *Education and Training*, 1969, pp. 83–84, report of the Secretary of Health, Education and Welfare to Congress on the MDTA.
(5): Bureau of National Affairs, *Daily Labor Report*, May 11, 1970, p. E–3.

Since OJT and JOBS are generally more successful than institutional training in providing employment, we may conclude that existing manpower programs as a whole do not succeed very well in removing bottlenecks, for they do not increase the effective supply of labor to those critical occupations classified as professional and technical. This undoubtedly results from the concern of these programs, especially that of the JOBS program, with training disadvantaged workers for low-skilled employment. It is by no means clear, furthermore, that the focus of the programs according to skill requirements is in any way sensitive to changes in the aggregate unemployment rate. If shifting the Phillips curve is to be a goal of manpower policy, changes in the aggregate unemployment rate should be used to direct changes in the allocation of training funds by occupation. In conclusion, it appears that manpower training has been excessively concentrated on entry-level jobs and has not been responsive to changes in shortage occupations.

An additional argument in favor of increasing the concentration of training money for more skilled work is the likely beneficial effect of such an increase on skill differentials in wages. Such a reallocation of training money would have the effect of increasing the supply of skilled workers relative to that of unskilled workers. This increase would in turn lower the wage of skilled workers relative to that of unskilled workers, assuming that there is no change in the relative demand for each type of labor.

Total Costs of Shifting the Curve

There are a number of reasons why we cannot get an exact numerical estimate of the resource cost of attempts to shift the short-run trade-off between inflation and unemployment. As mentioned earlier, we do not know the supply elasticities of labor between industries, between occupations, and between geographical areas. More important, we have only very rough estimates of the costs of training workers, and the majority of these estimates are based on government training programs. There is no reason to assume that these latter estimates are correct, for they may reflect inefficiencies in the training process. Finally, even if we knew all of these costs and parameters, we would still need to be able to predict the sectors of the economy in which bottlenecks would arise. While there is some hope of making such a prediction on the basis of observation of past business cycles, we could never achieve perfection in such a forecast.

We can, however, derive a lower bound for an estimate of the cost of shifting the curve by using a simple two-sector model. Consider an economy whose path is characterized by oscillations between two states: Period one, in which unemployment in sector A is nonexistent and unemployment in sector B is at the rate of 4 percent of the labor force in that sector; and period two, in which there is an excess demand for labor in sector A equal to 2 percent of its labor force and in which 2 percent of the labor force in sector B is unemployed. Assume further that the two sectors are of identical size in terms of the number of workers trained for employment in each sector and that between the two periods there are 5 percent entries to and exits from the labor force. (This corresponds roughly to the gross flows over one-half of a five-year trade cycle.)

If the labor force contains 80 million members, then our assumptions imply that there is an excess demand in period two for 0.8 million workers in sector A. The manpower training agency must train this many unemployed new workers so that they can apply for work during the second period in sector A and thus remove the bottleneck which causes wage inflation in our stylized economy. Assuming that the cost per man of such training lies between one thousand and ten thousand dollars, the total cost of such a program would lie between 0.8 billion and 8 billion dollars. This expenditure would be required initially to remove the bottleneck in the first period in which the training program is instituted. To ensure that the bottleneck does not arise in future even-numbered periods, the training agency must make sure that 1 percent of the new entrants to the labor force are trained in sector A. These new entrants must be trained so that they can replace existing workers who retire from the labor force. Continuing our assumption of a

2 percent annual attrition rate, the annual cost of keeping the economy free of this bottleneck ranges between $16 million and $160 million dollars. This is an expense that must be continued *ad infinitum.*

Our "estimate" of the total cost of shifting the Phillips curve is very much a lower limit to the true cost. Our figure of average per capita training expenditures assumes that no change in a workers' location is required. To overcome the immobility which gives rise to geographical bottlenecks would undoubtedly require a substantially greater expenditure. We also assume perfect certainty on the part of the training agency about the course of product demand and thus derived labor demand in each sector. In reality, there is no such certainty; and a government which wishes to be fairly sure of removing bottlenecks in the labor market must do substantial additional training in sectors in which there is some chance for these bottlenecks to arise.

Perhaps the grossest oversimplification in this informal model is its incorporation of only two sectors. There really are no isolated "sectors" in the economy, but rather a large number of different occupations in industries between which there are varying degrees of substitutability of labor. As aggregate demand increases over a business cycle, substantial excess demand for labor may arise in some occupations and slight excess demand in others; and there may be excess supply in a number of other industries and occupations. For this reason, we might expect bottlenecks to account for much more than 1 percent of the labor force in a time of relatively high aggregate demand.

For all of these reasons, our estimate of the cost of shifting the curve, both the initial cost averaging $4 billion and the annual maintenance cost of $90 million, are great understatements. The former sum is equal to total expenditures on training by the federal government through 1969.[27] (There is, of course, no assurance that these expenditures were used efficiently to achieve this goal.) Because our figure is an understatement, it seems clear that if removing bottlenecks and achieving a downward shift in the short-run Phillips curve form a goal of manpower policy, this goal requires significantly greater expenditures than have so far been made.

Financing the Shift

Assuming that optimal taxation implies benefit taxation, the appropriate means of financing training designed to shift the Phillips curve depends upon who benefits from the reduction in inflation at a given level of unemployment and who benefits from a reduction in unemployment at a given level of inflation. We compare the rates of inflation and unemployment chosen by the government in the short run, first in the case in which no training is given and then in the case in which training is offered. If the government were to choose the same rate of inflation in both cases but a higher rate of unemployment in the unsubsidized case, it is quite clear that the lower-income groups would stand to benefit from any training program. In this case, the effect of training is to provide jobs for those workers who are unemployed, presumably those who are least-skilled and whose incomes when they are employed are lowest. By the principle of benefit taxation, then, the lower-income workers should somehow finance the training program in this case. While it is clear that such financing cannot be made while they are unemployed, a program that involves taxing these workers' earnings during their period of employment might be used.

The other polar case is one in which the government chooses the same unemployment rate and uses the training program to ensure a lower rate of inflation. The question in this case is to determine which income classes benefit from the reduction in the rate of inflation. Table 4–10 presents a

Table 4–10. Spendable Incomes and the Rate of Inflation, 1965–1970

Month–Quarter	Annual Change, Consumer Price Index (Percent)	Manufacturing Production Workers' Weekly Spendable Earnings (1957–1959 Dollars)	Disposable Income in Billions (1958 Dollars)
March–I 1965	1.2	88.16	464.0
March–I 1966	2.8	87.80	497.5
March–I 1967	2.7	86.35	532.7
March–I 1968	3.9	88.28	575.0
March–I 1969	5.1	87.43	610.2
March–I 1970	6.1	86.22	659.9

Source: (1), (2): Bureau of National Affairs, *Daily Labor Report*, April 28, 1965; April 21, 1966; April 25, 1967; April 26, 1968; April 24, 1969; April 22, 1970.
(3): U.S. Department of Commerce, *Survey of Current Business*, January 1968; April 1970.

listing of the rate of inflation, real take-home pay of manufacturing production workers, and real disposable income for the economy as a whole. These data, while they may be confounded by changes in social security taxes during this period, indicate that during the period of relatively rapid inflation from 1965 to 1970, real spendable earnings of production workers, presumably middle-income individuals, decreased. This decline occurred simultaneously with a substantial rise in real disposable income in the economy, although part of the discrepancy between the two measures may be due to differences in measurement techniques. We may conclude that this inflation worked to the detriment of middle-income groups. There are several time-series regression studies which suggest further that the percentage of people living below a constant-dollar poverty line declines when inflation is more rapid, other things (mainly the unemployment rate) being equal.[28] If this experience is characteristic of a developed economy, the beneficiaries of a training program in this polar case would be the middle-classes, for they would no longer have to cope with the declining real spendable incomes which appear to accompany inflation. Benefit taxation in this case would suggest that these groups be taxed, probably by taxing their earnings, to finance the training programs which would produce this shift in the trade-off.

Unlike a number of cases in the area of public finance in which one can argue that both benefit taxation and ability-to-pay taxation produce the same indications for policy, in the case of training aimed at shifting the Phillips curve there is a fundamental conflict. The former approach to taxation suggests that middle-income groups should finance such a program, while the latter suggests that upper-income groups be made to pay. It is not our purpose here to discuss which approach should be taken. Our only aim is to point out that this conflict must be recognized if this goal is to be an important part of manpower policy.

Conclusions

In this chapter, we have attempted to provide some indications about the areas in which training should be offered if shifting the short-run trade-off between inflation and unemployment is a goal of manpower training policy. Our attempts to provide these indications and to discuss the costs of such a shift have been hampered by the great paucity of data and estimates of a number of essential parameters. It is vital to any training program we would like to operate in a rational manner that we acquire better estimates of the costs of training workers. These estimates should be made for a large number of occupational groups as well as for different industrial sectors of the economy. Without such estimates it is impossible to know the cost of a training program aimed at achieving this goal.

The elasticities of labor supply to different industries and occupations and the elasticities of substitution between different occupations must also be estimated if manpower training is to be used in a rational manner. While some attempts have been aimed toward providing estimates of the substitution elasticities, no supply elasticities have been estimated. Job ladders within plants must also be identified so that training programs may intervene at points which will ensure maximum additional hiring. Without such knowledge it is extremely difficult both to identify those sectors in which true bottlenecks exist in the labor market and to structure training programs that will produce the greatest beneficial secondary effects on employment.

The most concrete result of this chapter is its suggestion that training funds be concentrated more heavily in upgrading existing employees rather than in providing entry-level jobs. This approach is surely more efficient than training the unemployed for high-skilled jobs, for it entails training workers who already have some experience in a particular firm. Moreover, it is less likely to produce resentment on the part of currently employed workers who are passed over for promotion. The feedback effect discussed in Chapter 2 suggests that this strategy will help to avoid the possible curtailment of governmental appropriations which would arise from alternative policies and which might make the attainment of the goal of shifting the short-run Phillips curve more difficult.

5 Optimal Mobility and Other Aspects of Training in an Urban Economy

The multitude of endogenous variables in an urban economy, some of which are the spatial distribution of population, travel behavior, and flows of workers between jobs, are so interrelated that it makes little sense to concentrate on a detailed discussion of some aspect of the effects of manpower training on any one of these variables. Instead, we present analyses of the ways in which manpower training affects each of these three aspects of urban economic behavior. These discussions should provide some information on how training programs can be fashioned to change the structural parameters of an urban system in order to produce more desirable results.

The Goal of Manpower Training Policy in an Urban Area

Urban problems have in part been spurred by the rapid urbanization of the population in both the United States and other developed countries.[1] This and other changes in the geographic distribution of population have resulted in such difficulties as the lack of efficient transportation systems, the inability of the central cities to finance adequate government services, and residential racial segregation. While manpower policy might seem to be of some use in solving these urban problems, it was not mentioned for this purpose during the discussions which laid the foundations for manpower training programs in the United States. There is no sign that considerations of urban problems affected the drafting of early manpower legislation, nor was urban policy discussed in the hearings and debates on manpower legislation in 1962.

During the middle 1960s, however, the goal of using manpower policy as a means of combating urban ills came under discussion. One observer attributes this change in the direction of policy to a growing recognition that manpower training could improve "the threatening and increasingly complex urban crisis."[2] By 1970, America's mayors had recognized the importance of manpower problems in the urban crisis, and, at the federal level, this was acknowledged by the devotion of the rapidly expanding JOBS program to urban areas and its neglect of rural and small-town problems.[3] However, rather than being used to help remove the underlying problems peculiar to

95

all urban areas regardless of their demographic composition, urban manpower policy has been directed solely toward helping the poor, especially the non-white poor. The proposed 1968 amendments to the MDTA were designed "to provide meaningful public and private employment opportunities which would relieve severe unemployment and underemployment in both urban and rural areas." These areas were defined as ones which "contain high concentrations or proportions of low income families and individuals."[4]

There are a number of more general aspects of urban policy which might be explicitly related to manpower policy. Moreover, these are areas in which a properly administered urban manpower policy might well complement and enhance the value of other aspects of public programs. Most labor mobility occurs within a specific urban area. If mobility does not take place at an optimal rate, this failure may be an important indication of the inefficient operation of urban labor-market institutions. Manpower training and in-formation services will affect these flows of workers between jobs in an urban area, and both this effect and the meaning of optimal mobility are worthy of more detailed economic investigation.

A number of observers have linked the lack of employment opportunities for nonwhites to the inefficient and sometimes even unavailable transportation between their residences and potential places of employment.[5] In recognition of this problem some OJT contracts have actually entailed innovative means of transporting ghetto residents to suburban job locations.[6] In addition to the effects of the relationship between these two factors on the ghetto population, training and transportation policies interact to affect all inhabitants of an urban area. The amount of training embodied in an individual affects his likelihood of seeking employment and entering the labor force, while the availability of cheap and rapid transportation between his residence and potential jobs influences his interest in investing in his own training. This relationship holds not just for disadvantaged workers, but for any person who must commute to work and simultaneously maintain his ability to function effectively in employment.

The fiscal position of the central cities of metropolitan areas has been consistently eroded over the past decades by the emigration of both employment and the more affluent citizens of these areas. Between 1959 and 1967, median family income in the central cities of urbanized areas rose by 16 percent, while the comparable figure for the suburbs of their central cities was 21 percent. This widening of suburban–central-city differentials continued a trend observed between 1949 and 1959. There is also evidence that employment opportunities have been increasing more rapidly in the suburbs than in the central cities and even that the rate of suburbanization of jobs has exceeded that of population.[7] While it is not clear whether this migration is due to changes in the relative locational advantages of the central city as opposed to the suburbs or to conscious governmental policy which has favored the suburbs, the direction of flow is indisputable. An important matter to consider is the potential effects of training programs aimed primarily at disadvantaged workers on these flows of employment and residents. If one effect of such programs is to raise some poor workers into the middle-class, encouraging them to move from the city and leaving the poorest residents remaining, then perhaps training programs should be redirected to avoid this detrimental secondary effect.

A Model of Urban Labor Mobility

In this section, we build an economic model of the determinants of intercity differences in the amount of voluntary mobility in the labor force. By voluntary mobility we mean the percentage of employed workers who quit their jobs in a given month. This quit rate is an indicator of the degree to which labor-market institutions in a city enable workers to choose to change jobs as the relative attractiveness of different jobs varies.

Our results can be used to discover which cities and urban areas have unusually high or low mobility once other determinants of mobility are fully accounted for. This information should be useful in steering manpower training resources toward cities in which they are most needed. For example, if mobility in an urban area is unusually low, we may conclude that there are characteristics of the labor market which might be ameliorated by programs aimed at increasing information and removing labor-market rigidities. Similarly, urban areas with unusually high mobility may be those in which labor-market institutions lead to excessive turnover and where training and information programs might be concentrated to reduce interfirm flows of labor. The designation of areas with unusual mobility patterns and a discussion of what constitutes optimal mobility are left for the next section.

There is a long history of interest among labor economists in patterns of labor mobility both across industries and across geographical areas. Within the category of interindustry labor mobility two strands of thought have been pursued. Some studies have analyzed this mobility on a nationwide basis; others have discussed how the aggregate amount of voluntary mobility differs among urban areas.[8] The purpose of the first strand of research, which has received by far the greater bulk of attention in recent years, has been to test the competitive hypothesis that wage differentials affect flows of labor.[9] In any case of labor-market disequilibrium, industries with high wages should be those to which workers from other industries flow and whose own workers have a low propensity to leave their current employment. Even in equilibrium, high-wage industries where specific training is important will exhibit lower rates of exit by their employees. Similarly, in industries with unusually low wages, we should expect to find substantial outflows of labor to other, high-paying, industries.

Additional interest in interindustry differences in voluntary mobility centers on the extent to which the demographic characteristics of labor affect mobility patterns. Using human capital theory, we can generate and test hypotheses about how these characteristics affect the quit rate. This provides a useful indirect test of the validity of this part of labor-market theory, and it enables us to isolate demographic groups which are characterized by unusually high mobility and whose labor-market behavior needs greater attention from manpower policy.

The study of intercity differences in the amount of interindustry mobility has been greatly neglected during the last twenty years. This lack of attention is especially unfortunate because the rapid increases in the amount of data available and the greater sophistication in the econometrics used to analyze those data could provide substantial new insights into these problems. This information could have been especially useful in our understanding of how urban labor markets operate and might have provided some important policy information to improve their operation. The work in this section attempts to fill this gap in the analysis of mobility within labor markets.

An analysis of differences in mobility across cities may be more useful from both an analytical and policy standpoint than a discussion of inter-industry mobility in an entire economy. The bulk of voluntary mobility takes place within rather than between metropolitan areas. Because of the great psychic and pecuniary costs involved in changing residence, the major fixity in a labor market is not to an occupation or an industry, but rather to a geographical area. The urban area is, therefore, a more appropriate unit within which to analyze mobility than is the nation as a whole.

Consider a utility-maximizing worker in an urban labor market who is employed in a plant in the area. He will quit for another job if the discounted value of its utility stream is greater than that in his present employment. Since during his early period of employment in his current job he may have invested in some specific training in himself, his wage in that job will be higher than an alternative wage in other labor-market opportunities.[10] For that reason, we should expect that workers in firms in which specific training is important have lower propensities to quit than workers who have not made these investments in themselves. Because we have no available direct measure of specific training, we use as a proxy for it the wage rate in the city. If firms bear part of the costs of such training, they will maintain higher wages in order to avoid incurring excessive training costs. Cities in which real wages are higher will be those in which firms and workers have undertaken more investment in specific training, and they will therefore be characterized by lower quit rates when we abstract from intercity demographic differences.

In comparing alternative utility streams, the worker must take into account the possibility of a period without work while he either searches for another job or drops out of the labor market after quitting his present one. A longer period of unemployment lowers the discounted value of the expected stream of returns in other jobs. If the city is characterized by substantial amounts of unemployment, the average worker considering the possibility of quitting can expect to spend much time in the pool of unemployed workers. For that reason, we expect a city to have lower voluntary mobility when unemployment is high than when it is low.[11]

In an urban area characterized by a rapid influx of new migrants, we might expect the rate of voluntary mobility to be higher than in areas into which this flow does not take place. Individuals acquire substantial information about job opportunities in the labor markets in which they live over the course of their lifetimes. If a person moves to a new labor market, he must spend some period of time searching for and trying out new jobs in order to acquire information about opportunities in his new home.[12] Voluntary mobility by new migrants is thus an investment which raises their earnings in the future.

If we base our theory on rational economic behavior, we can isolate a number of demographic variables which might also have an effect on intercity differences in voluntary mobility. Younger workers will exhibit higher rates of mobility, for youth may be viewed as a time in which individuals quit jobs frequently in order to gather information about the labor market.[13] Women may also have higher quit rates. Because they are likely to drop out of the labor force in order to raise families, we should expect them to have invested less in their own specific training.[14] Finally, there is some evidence that nonwhites may exhibit higher voluntary quit rates when other factors are taken into account.[15] All three of these demographic hypotheses can be tested using this model of mobility in urban labor markets.

Having considered both the economic and demographic determinants of intercity differences in the quit rate, we may still find random factors which cannot be explained by specific characteristics of the cities. Such nonmeasurable factors as the amount of job information available to workers and the amount of employer monopsony power may well produce unexplained differences in mobility across cities. It is these factors that we wish to isolate and which may be of use in directing manpower policy to cities which exhibit either very high or very low residual variation in voluntary mobility. We assume, therefore, that the error term in the equations we estimate reflects these problems.

This theoretical discussion suggests that we estimate the following equations.

$$q = \alpha_0 + \alpha_1 WAGE + \alpha_2 MIGR + \alpha_3 UMP + \alpha_4 YOUTH + \alpha_5 NONW$$
$$+ \alpha_6 FEMALE + \varepsilon \qquad (5.1)$$

$$q = \alpha_0' + \alpha_1' WAGE + \alpha_2' MIGR + \alpha_3' UMP + \varepsilon' \qquad (5.2)$$

where the variable names are self-explanatory and ε and ε' are stochastic disturbance terms. Equation (5.2) is estimated in order to determine whether the demographic characteristics as a whole have any significant effect on intercity differences in mobility.

In reality we cannot assume that the wage is exogenous in equations (5.1) and (5.2). Instead, it is likely to be affected by some of the demographic factors determining the quit rate as well as by other variables such as industrial concentration and the extent of unionization in the city. We should therefore estimate a two-equation system consisting of either equation (5.1) or (5.2) and $WAGE = F(X)$, where X is a vector of variables, not including q, which affect the wage level in a city. This equation and one of the quits equations form a simultaneous system with a triangular matrix of coefficients of the endogenous variables $WAGE$ and q. If we make the assumption that the error terms are not correlated across the two equations, we can conclude that the system is recursive. Without any specific reasons for this correlation to exist our assumption is fairly reasonable. We can thus proceed to estimate equations (5.1) and (5.2) with some confidence that ordinary least squares estimates are free of simultaneous equations bias.[16]

Equations (5.1) and (5.2) are estimated for both 1964 and 1969. The former year is used in order to achieve greater comparability with the demographic data derived from the 1960 Census of Population. It is furthermore a year of relatively high aggregate unemployment, and the parameter estimates for that year should differ from those based on data from 1969, a year of low aggregate unemployment. Data are available for 1964 from fifty-eight labor market areas listed in Table 5–1. These areas include 65 percent of the total population of standard metropolitan statistical areas in the United States. For 1969, data on the quit rate for twelve of the areas used in the 1964 sample are not available, but there are data for six new areas. The sample for 1969 thus contains fifty-two areas.

Table 5–1. Labor Markets in the Urban Mobility Sample

Birmingham, Ala.	New York, N.Y.
Phoenix, Ariz.	Rochester, N.Y.
San Diego, Calif.[a]	Syracuse, N.Y.
San Francisco–Oakland, Calif.[a]	Utica–Rome, N.Y.
San Jose, Calif.[a]	Greensboro–High Point, N.C.
Denver, Colo.[b]	Akron, Ohio
Bridgeport, Conn.[a]	Canton, Ohio
Hartford, Conn.	Cincinnati, Ohio
New Haven, Conn.[a]	Cleveland, Ohio
Wilmington, Del.	Columbus, Ohio
Washington, D.C.	Dayton, Ohio
Miami, Fla.	Toledo, Ohio
Atlanta, Ga.	Younstown–Warren, Ohio
Chicago, Ill.[b]	Portland, Ore.
Indianapolis, Ind.	Allentown–Bethlehem–Easton, Pa.
Wichita, Kan.	Lancaster, Pa.
Louisville, Ky.	Philadelphia, Pa.
New Orleans, La.	Pittsburgh, Pa.
Baltimore, Md.	Reading, Pa.
Boston, Mass.	Wilkes–Barre–Hazleton, Pa.
Springfield–Chicopee–Holyoke, Mass.[a]	York, Pa.
Worcester, Mass.[a]	Providence–Pawtucket, R.I.
Detroit, Mich.	Greenville, S.C.[b]
Minneapolis–St. Paul, Minn.	Chattanooga, Tenn.[a]
Kansas City, Mo.	Memphis, Tenn.
St. Louis, Mo.	Nashville, Tenn.[a]
Jersey City, N.J.[b]	Dallas, Texas[a]
Newark, N.J.[b]	Fort Worth, Texas[a]
Paterson–Clifton–Passaic, N.J.[b]	Houston, Texas[a]
Albany–Schenectady–Troy, N.Y.	Richmond, Va.
Binghamton, N.Y.	Seattle–Everett, Wash.
Buffalo, N.Y.	Milwaukee, Wis.

[a] This area is only included in the 1964 sample.
[b] This area is only included in the 1969 sample.

The quit rate is the percentage of manufacturing employees who leave a plant voluntarily during a given month, and the wage variable is the average weekly earnings of manufacturing production workers. We should use some cost-of-living measure in order to deflate this money wage to real terms and thus provide a closer link between our estimates and the theory of labor mobility. Unfortunately such data are not available for most of the labor markets in our sample, and we therefore ignore this problem. This neglect may lead to an underestimate of the absolute value of the elasticity of quits with respect to wages if real wages are correlated with the cost of living across cities.[17]

The migration data are the percent of families resident in the area in 1960 who lived in another county in 1955. This is admittedly only a proxy for true migration during the sample period, as there may be substantial changes in flows of population between 1960 and our two sample periods. The *FEMALE* and *YOUTH* variables are simply the percentages of the labor force accounted for by these demographic groups. The variable *NONW* is based upon the entire population of the area rather than simply the labor force, because a racial breakdown of the labor force is not available.[18] Table 5–2 lists the

Table 5–2. Simple Correlations Between the Variables in the Urban Mobility Model

	WAGE	*MIGR*	*UMP*	*YOUTH*	*NONW*	*FEMALE*
				1964		
q	−.66*	.41*	−.16	.12	.21	.56*
WAGE		.08	−.08	−.10	−.04	−.72*
MIGR			−.02	.54*	.23	−.08
UMP				.07	−.31*	−.32*
YOUTH					.04	−.26
NONW						.20
				1969		
q	−.57*	.43*	−.17	.43*	.11	.52*
WAGE		−.07	.02	−.10	−.09	−.63*
MIGR			−.08	.41*	.25	.18
UMP				−.36*	−.02	−.13
YOUTH					.17	.18
NONW						.20

* Significant at the 1 percent level of confidence.

matrices of simple correlation coefficients among the seven variables in the model.

Table 5–3 presents estimates of the models in equations (5.1) and (5.2) for both 1964 and 1969. In 1964, all of the economic variables have coefficients which are significantly different from zero and have the signs predicted by our theory. None of the coefficients of the demographic variables is significant, and a comparison of equation (5.1) to (5.2) shows that as a group they contribute little to explaining variations across cities in the quit rate in 1964. All of the economic variables, *WAGE*, *MIGR* and *UMP*, have coefficients with the expected signs; and, except for those on the unemployment rate in 1969, all are significantly different from zero.

In order to test whether the estimates of the parameters in these models are efficient, we use a test for heteroscedasticity proposed by Goldfeld and

Table 5–3. Estimates of Equations (5.1) and (5.2) for 1964 and 1969

Variable	64.1	Equation 64.2	69.1	69.2
Constant	3.4594^a	3.4848^a	0.8939	4.9938^a
	(1.3634)^b	(0.2883)	(2.1190)	(0.6571)
WAGE	−0.0204^a	−0.0210^a	−0.0166^a	−0.0211^a
	(0.0037)	(0.0022)	(0.0051)	(0.0040)
MIGR	0.0314^a	0.0294^a	0.0317^a	0.0421^a
	(0.0060)	(0.0048)	(0.0124)	(0.0114)
UMP	−0.0760^a	−0.0814^a	−0.0304	−0.1193
	(0.0366)	(0.0294)	(0.0988)	(0.0944)
YOUTH	−0.0129	—	0.1061^a	—
	(0.0206)		(0.0517)	
NONW	0.0002	—	−0.0061	—
	(0.0043)		(0.0085)	
FEMALE	0.0035	—	0.0519	—
	(0.0245)		(0.0416)	
R^2	0.7006	0.6975	0.5532	0.4926
σ_ε	0.2578	0.2518	0.5118	0.5281
$N =$	58	58	52	52

^{a} Significantly different from zero at the 10 percent level.
^{b} Standard errors in parentheses.

Quandt.[19] In particular, if there is some relation between population size in the metropolitan areas and the absolute value of the estimated residuals in equations (5.1) and (5.2), we should adjust for this fact in our estimation procedure. Performing a test based on the number of peaks in a set of residuals ordered by population size, we find that in none of the four equations is the number of peaks different from what one would expect if the residuals were randomly distributed according to population size of the cities. In short, we cannot reject the hypothesis of homoscedasticity, and we may conclude that ordinary least squares is providing us with efficient estimates of the parameters in our models, at least as regards this one possible source of inefficiency.

Although our chief intention is to analyze intercity differences in mobility, our results for the urban sample have interesting implications in comparison to results obtained using industry data. Table 5–4 lists estimates of the elasticities of the quit rate with respect to both wages and the unemployment rate. Comparing the estimates for the elasticity with respect to wages, we find that the values based on data from urban areas correspond quite closely to those based on industry data for the entire economy. We may conclude

Table 5–4. Comparisons of Alternative Estimates of the Elasticities of Voluntary Mobility with Respect to Wages and Unemployment

			Equation		
	64.1	64.2	69.1	69.2	Industry Data
$E(q, WAGE)$	-1.71	-1.75	-0.94	-1.20	-1.07[a]
$E(q, UMP)$	-0.26	-0.28	-0.04	-0.15	-1.81[b]

[a] Based on estimates using industry data for 1950 and 1960 by John Pencavel, *An Analysis of the Quit Rate in American Manufacturing Industry* (Princeton, N.J.: Industrial Relations Section, 1970), pp. 30, 61, and 65.

[b] Arithmetic mean of elasticities $E(q_i, UMP)$ based on time-series regressions for each of 28 four-digit manufacturing and industries, 1958–1966. (Daniel Hamermesh, "A Disaggregative Econometric Model of Gross Changes in Employment," *Yale Economic Essays* 9 (Fall 1969): 123.

that these results are fairly good evidence that the elasticity of quits with respect to wages is approximately unity.

The estimated unemployment elasticities are much lower in the cross section in our model than is the elasticity based on an average of time-series estimates. This difference may be attributable to the use of internally consistent data in the time series and the possibility that the cross-section data we have used on the unemployment rate are not comparable across cities. An economic reason is that workers in high unemployment labor markets may become used to a fairly high level of unemployment. Quit behavior may be determined not by the unemployment rate itself, but rather by deviations from some "permanent" unemployment rate. In the time-series regression this problem does not exist, for any change in the aggregate unemployment rate is necessarily a deviation from the permanent unemployment rate. If workers do react to unemployment in this fashion, we should then expect to find the observed high negative elasticity in the time series and fairly low estimates of the cross-section elasticity.

The amount of immigration to the city produces the expected positive effect on the quit rate, but this effect is not quite so significant in 1969 as in the estimates for 1964. Part of this difference may be due merely to problems with the data, for the 1960 data may be a poor proxy for migration into the city in the years just preceding 1969. This difficulty may be less acute when we use the 1960 data in the 1964 regressions.

The *YOUTH* variable produces the expected significant positive effect on the quit rate in 1969, and the *FEMALE* variable has a positive but insignificant effect in both samples. These results corroborate previous estimates based on interindustry differences in voluntary mobility. The

NONW variable, however, has a negative effect in one year and a positive effect in the other. While nonwhites may very well have higher rates of quitting than whites, these differences appear attributable to their other demographic characteristics, especially their high rate of geographic mobility (see Table 5–2).

Optimal Mobility and the Use of Manpower Programs

It is impossible to set forth a generally agreed upon definition of the optimal rate of voluntary mobility of labor in an urban area.[20] Management officials undoubtedly believe that any rate of mobility which conflicts with production scheduling is too high. Union officials would be much less willing to acknowledge the possibility that excess turnover exists. The Japanese experience with wage increases determined by length of service suggests that optimal mobility could be defined as that which is low enough to allow firms and individuals to engage in long-range planning for the individual's future with the firm.[21] Such planning could induce substantially greater investment in the worker than is now possible, given our rates of interfirm mobility. Manpower policies oriented to this definition would result in a faster accumulation of human capital and thus a higher per capita income in the future.

In the context of a Western economy we can construct a typology of cases of "bad" mobility and relate these to alternative manpower programs which would ameliorate them. First, consider Case I, that of excessively *high* mobility. One example of this is the worker who quits a job providing a steady progression in wages and steady improvement in skills for another job where the initial wage is high but no advancement is possible. If the worker has a high rate of time preference, this move is entirely consistent with lifetime utility maximization; yet social welfare might be greater (because the initial investment in hiring this worker would not be lost and total investment in him over his working life would be greater) if he stayed in his first job. In this case of a divergence of the private from the social optimum, a program which provides subsidies to firms that do substantial upgrading would help to decrease excess turnover because the subsidized firm would be induced to pay higher wages to workers being upgraded.

A different form of Case I occurs when workers quit their current jobs in order to search for more satisfactory employment when none exists. This type of mobility is the result of the inadequate dissemination of information on the state of the labor market in the particular urban area. Excessive mobility in this case can be reduced by programs such as Job Banks which increase workers' knowledge of employment alternatives.

Case II is that of excessively *low* mobility arising from a divergence between social and private rates of time preference. One example involves workers who do not leave their current jobs for other employment which would provide a larger discounted lifetime utility stream if the foregone wages needed to pay for training in the new jobs did not have to be considered. An obvious example of this is an older worker in a small, declining firm who, even aside from possible age discrimination, will not move because he does not wish to forego the benefits that have accrued to him because of his seniority. Because his rate of time preference is greater than society's, it may be worthwhile for society to offer this type of worker retraining allowances to help raise mobility closer to an optimum rate. The other example of Case II is that of workers locked into jobs because of inadequate knowledge of better job opportunities in other firms. This difficulty, like its converse under Case I, can be remedied by programs which increase the amount of information available in the labor market.

This typology illustrates that mobility may be too high or too low depending on the reasons motivating individual workers to quit or remain on their jobs. Indeed, we have seen that the divergence between private and social rates of time preference can produce overly high or low mobility depending on the circumstances. We cannot determine whether mobility in an economy is excessive (characterized by Case I) or insufficient (as in Case II). We can, however, conclude that in cities with unusually high mobility, i.e., where the residuals based on the coefficients in equations (5.1) and (5.2) are large and positive, manpower policy should concentrate on programs such as those discussed under Case I. Contrarywise, those programs discussed under Case II should, *ceteris paribus*, be restricted to urban areas in which mobility is unusually low, i.e., in which the residuals are large and negative.

In Table 5–5, we present estimates of the average residual for each of the four major regions in each of the equations we have estimated. None of these average residuals is significantly different from zero, and in the case of the South there is no consistent evidence as to the sign. The residuals for the North Central region are nearly as large as their standard error in 1969 but are nearly zero in 1964. The residuals for the West are consistently positive and almost as large as their standard error, while those for the Northeast are consistently negative. These results imply that there may be factors in urban areas in the West which result in unusually high voluntary mobility, while some factors in the Northeast result in unusually low labor mobility. Assuming that the Northeast is a high cost-of-living region and that the cost of living in the West is relatively low, we may conclude that our results do not adequately reflect differences in the residuals between these two regions.

Table 5–5. Average Residuals by Region, 1964 and 1969, Equations (5.1) and (5.2)

	Northeast	South	North Central	West
			Region	
			1964	
(5.1)	−.0481	.0245	.0084	.0818
	(.0562)[a]	(.0644)	(.0666)	(.1052)
(5.2)	−.0482	.0300	.0033	.0801
	(.0549)	(.0629)	(.0650)	(.1028)
$N_j =$	21[b]	16	15	6
			1969	
(5.1)	−.0799	−.0288	.0898	.1263
	(.1144)	(.1477)	(.1279)	(.2558)
(5.2)	−.0958	−.0760	.1354	.1641
	(.1181)	(.1524)	(.1320)	(.2640)
$N_j =$	20	12	16	4

[a] Standard error of the average residual in parentheses is $\sigma_\varepsilon / \sqrt{N_j}$.
[b] $N_j =$ number of observations.

Were we able to use real wages rather than money wages, we would find a more significant positive average residual in the West and a more significant negative one in the Northeast.[22] We would also discover that the average residuals in the South (with a low cost of living) and in the North Central area (with a relatively high cost of living) are nearly zero.

One might conjecture that the positive average residual for the West (a high-migration area) is due to our failure to include a quadratic term for *MIGR* in equations (5.1) and (5.2). If it were included and had a significant positive effect on quit behavior, the average residual in the West would decrease toward zero. One basis for including it would be that migrants group together to create a restless culture in an area. If this hypothesis were correct, doubling the percentage of recent migrants would more than double the average quit rate in a labor market. In actuality, the addition of $MIGR^2$ to the equations has only a minute effect on the residuals. In 1964, the coefficients for this variable are positive but have t values less than 0.4, while in 1969 the coefficients are actually negative (but also with very low t values).

Various urban areas appear to have consistently high or low rates of mobility. While this finding has been demonstrated in earlier work, the results in our equations are the first to take account of specific demographic or economic factors and link unusual *residual* mobility patterns to the efficiency of labor market institutions in the areas. Many of the areas with large negative or positive residuals listed in Table 5–6 in 1969 are also those

Table 5–6. Urban Areas with Unusually High or Low Voluntary Labor Mobility, 1964 and 1969

Area[a]	1964 Residual in (5.2)[b]	Area	1969 Residual in (5.2)[b]
Providence, R.I.	0.550	Atlanta, Ga.	1.148
Houston, Texas[c]	0.438	Greenville, S.C.[d]	1.015
Portland, Ore.	0.427	Providence, R.I.	0.996
York, Pa.	0.385	Chicago, Ill.[d]	0.963
Fort Worth, Texas[c]	0.360	York, Pa.	0.740
Seattle, Wash.	0.351	Detroit, Mich.	0.663
Worcester, Mass.[c]	0.325	Toledo, Ohio	0.574
Greensboro, N.C.	0.299	Miami, Fla.	0.547
Detroit, Mich.	0.294	Portland, Ore.	0.530
Albany, N.Y.	−0.484	Pittsburgh, Pa.	−0.918
Richmond, Va.	−0.407	Richmond, Va.	−0.867
Columbus, Ohio	−0.378	Washington, D.C.	−0.842
Chattanooga, Tenn.[c]	−0.364	Wilmington, Del.	−0.768
Utica, N.Y.	−0.347	Binghamton, N.Y.	−0.651
Philadelphia, Pa.	−0.314	Wilkes-Barre, Pa.	−0.571
Allentown, Pa.	−0.311		

[a] Only the major city in each labor-market area is listed.
[b] Absolute value of the residual for the area is greater than σ_ε in both equation (5.1) and (5.2).
[c] This area is only included in the 1964 sample.
[d] This area is only included in the 1969 sample.

which were characterized by similarly high or low residuals in 1964. (This is especially true of the areas with unusually high positive residuals.) We may conclude that these areas have consistently unusual degrees of mobility, and that they should be the targets for cost-effective manpower programs designed to change existing mobility patterns. In both groups, the amount and quality of labor-market information should be improved. In those in the top part of Table 5–6 programs which decrease turnover, such as upgrading subsidies, should be used; manpower policies which provide workers with retraining allowances should be especially concentrated in cities in the bottom part of Table 5–6.

If we view the quit rate as being affected by the wage because the latter is a measure of specific training, we can imagine that changes in the amount of training offered will produce changes in the quit rate. Thus government subsidies to increase upgrading will increase the amount of training offered and indirectly lower the turnover rate. While the exact costs of producing any increase in the quit rate cannot be measured, we can measure the magnitude of the wage increase required to lower the quit rate by a given amount.

Assume that the costs of raising the average wage in an area by increasing training are directly proportional to the size of the labor force in the area, but that the costs increase quadratically with the size of the wage increase needed. It can easily be shown that: (1) These assumptions imply that funds be spent in each area in an amount proportional to its labor force. And (2) the required absolute change in wages is identical across areas and is equal to $a/\hat{\alpha}_1$, where a is the desired change in the quit rate and $\hat{\alpha}_1$ is the estimate of the wage parameter in equations (5.1) and (5.2).

In Table 5–7 we list the average wage increases needed to produce a one-

Table 5–7. Wage Changes Required to Lower the Average Quit Rate by One-Half Percentage Point

| | Equation | | | |
	64.1	64.2	69.1	69.2
Average quit rate	1.3	1.3	2.4	2.4
Average weekly wage	$108.64	$108.64	$136.30	$136.30
Required change in wage	+$24.51	+$23.81	+$23.69	+$30.12

half percentage-point decline in the monthly quit rate. These increases in wages are not due to price-level changes, nor are they the result of changes in real wages arising from movement along some growth path. Rather, they state the required wage increase resulting from an increase in the stock of specific training given the existing amounts of physical capital and general training. As such, one must infer from the very large magnitudes in Table 5–7 that attempts to produce a significant drop in turnover rates through increasing upgrading would probably have to be very costly.

A Simple Two-Class Model of Training and Transportation

In addition to their effects on labor mobility, manpower programs are also linked to travel behavior in an urban area. Many programs designed to provide training opportunities for nonwhite residents of central cities have failed because of inadequate urban transportation systems. High dropout rates from the on-the-job courses in these programs have been attributed to the long and costly trips from the central-city residential ghettoes to the suburban plants where the training takes place. Indeed, there is some evidence that ghettoization per se lowers the rate of labor-force participation.[23] It is apparent that "training, education, counseling, placement and transportation programs complement one another."[24] This complementarity exists not only for the specific case of disadvantaged individuals, but also for the entire process of training and transportation in an urban area. Because of the generality of this relationship, a market-wide policy for training and transportation should be developed in order to ensure that the side effects of one specific policy do not vitiate the positive direct effects of another policy. While the actual mix of policies depends on the empirical values of individual parameters, we can outline the ways in which training and transportation interact and conditions under which alternative policy strategies will be successful.

Assume that there are two classes of workers living in the area, and that all jobs are located at some point F. All the upper-income residents live together at a point d_U miles away from F; and all lower-income residents live at another point d_L miles from F. The assumption that residential location and distance to work are fixed is the usual one in discussing demand for transportation in an urban area.[25] In considering policy conclusions, we should remember the drawbacks of this assumption, which is really applicable only in the short run. We further postulate that all members of group U (upper income) have sufficient prior training embodied in them to qualify for the high-skilled jobs in which vacancies exist. All members of group U are, therefore, assumed to be either employed in high-skilled jobs or not in the labor force. We assume that members of the low-income group L are either employed in low-skilled jobs, unemployed, or not in the labor force.

These assumptions restrict the government to choosing some combination from among three policy alternatives: (1) T_U, provides improved transportation for group U to jobs where they are located. By lowering travel time, this strategy increases the net wage of members of this group and thus raises their propensity to participate in the labor force. (2) T_L, provides transportation for lower-income residents and thus increases their labor-force participation rate. (3) M_L, provides training opportunities for unemployed members of group L which enable them to fill vacancies in the high-skilled jobs that are the only ones in which vacancies exist. This last strategy affects levels of employment in the city by providing trained workers for vacant jobs, and it has the indirect effect of increasing labor-force participation in group L. This latter effect is the result of entry into the labor force in response to the decrease in the unemployment rate in group L produced by the training program. These last two strategies are a paradigm of a successful training and transportation scheme for the disadvantaged. They train the unemployed only for jobs in which post-training employment is a certainty and in which they will not be displacing incumbent employees. They also provide expenditures for transporting the newly trained workers to their jobs.

The optimal mix of strategies depends on the goals which the society wishes to pursue. In this section, we consider only two possibilities: (1) The government seeks to increase E_L, employment in the lower-income group; or (2) it seeks to raise employment in the entire community, i.e., in both income groups. We consider only goals relating to employment and ignore the possibility that the government may instead wish to concentrate on raising income levels. Although these two types of goals are clearly related, the generation of new employment opportunities is a more direct and easily traceable consequence of improved training and transportation than are increased incomes. Limiting the discussion to employment goals has the additional advantage that we can concentrate on the utilization of idle labor rather than on the more complex problem of analyzing income changes among existing employed workers.

We consider conditions under which each of the three strategies will be more or less successful in achieving the two alternative goals we have outlined. We assume that the government has fixed resources available to it and that it therefore seeks to achieve the particular goal as inexpensively as possible. If the goal is to increase E_L alone, there are certain conditions which produce the result that T_U is the most efficient strategy. Two parameters must be considered: the change in labor-force participation of group U with respect to changes in T_U and the degree to which high- and low-skilled jobs are complements in production. Money spent in improving transportation for upper-income groups increases labor-force participation and thus employment in high-skilled occupations. If the two occupation classes are strongly complementary, this reduction in high-skilled job vacancies will increase the demand for low-income residents to fill low-skilled jobs. If spending additional dollars on strategy T_U produces a much greater per dollar increase in participation of members of group U than dollars spent on T_L produce in group L, the strategy T_U becomes even more attractive than the two alternatives. One major factor is the relative cost of land lying on the paths between the city's factories (at location F) and each of the two income groups. As the land between F and U becomes relatively less expensive than that between F and L, strategy T_U increases in desirability. The relative magnitudes of d_U and d_L should also be taken into account. As d_U becomes smaller, increasing numbers of high-income residents can be induced to enter the labor force for relatively small expenditures on improved transportation. Travel time along d_U can be driven very low, and, if the two occupation classes are complementary, increased demand for the labor of group L individuals will increase employment in that group.

Whether the conditions exist that make improved transportation for upper-income groups the most efficient way of increasing employment among lower-income individuals is very difficult to determine. The optimal strategy depends on the responsiveness of the labor-force participation of each group to equal declines in travel time; on land values and the residential location of each group relative to job location in the area; and on the average complementarity of skills in production in the area. There is no direct evidence on the first two of these three conditions, but there is some empirical work suggesting very tentatively that different occupational categories are nearly perfect substitutes in production.[26] Despite this fragmentary evidence, to the extent that the other two conditions are valid, a society which wishes to increase employment for disadvantaged urban residents might well consider improving transportation for middle- and upper-income groups.

If the goal of society is to increase total employment, the same parameters as those discussed above should be considered in determining which training or transportation strategy is most appropriate. Under our assumptions that there is no unemployment in group U and that nonparticipants in that group have the training necessary for high-skilled jobs, T_U is most efficient in increasing employment in group U. Any combination of strategies T_L and M_L will have as its initial effect an increase in labor-force participation of L and will produce no increase in the supply of trained members of group U. Since T_U is always the appropriate strategy to use to increase employment in group U, the same conditions which ensure its superiority in increasing employment of L must also make it the most efficient strategy for increasing employment in the entire community.

As we noted above, employer and residential location are not fixed in the long run; our tentative policy conclusions are thus most appropriately applied in the short run. In the long run, the subsidy strategy T_U would cause some upper-income residents to move their residences further away from their current places of employment. Firms that are especially dependent on the labor supplied by upper-income individuals would have an incentive to move to cities where this subsidy is offered. Whether the resource costs of these distortions in location decisions outweigh the short-run benefits produced by the subsidy is purely an empirical question.

This simple model relating residential location to transportation and training is much too general to produce any explicit guides which could lead to changes in specific policies. Rather, it is intended to demonstrate that both training and transportation policies work through the mechanism of changing labor-force participation to affect employment in an urban area. To some extent, manpower training programs and improved transportation systems are alternative policies which produce similar effects, and it may be that in some cities problems now being attacked by one method could be solved more efficiently by the other.

The Effects of Training Ghetto Residents on the Distribution of Population in an Urban Area

Another important question is the extent to which the policy of helping disadvantaged workers in central cities has had a spillover effect both on their locational decisions and on those of other residents of the central cities. If this manpower policy strategy has the effect of inducing the most able disadvantaged workers to leave the central cities, we must conclude that it will be responsible for a further increase in the serious fiscal problems of the central cities. The extent to which this will occur depends upon a number of parameters which we discuss below.

Assume that an urban area is divided into a central city and a suburban ring, and that individuals choose their residential location based upon the income of other persons already residing in either of these two areas. The actual direction of this effect depends upon individual tastes in residential choice. One hypothesis is that individuals choose to live near people with similar incomes and tastes in order to obtain a mix of public services which they find desirable. (In the public finance literature this is known as the Tiebout hypothesis.[27] Although Tiebout was mainly interested in the effects of this hypothesis on the demand for publicly produced goods, much attention in the literature has focused on its implications for the theory of residential location.) The opposite hypothesis, that people choose to live near individuals with incomes and tastes substantially different from theirs, hardly seems tenable. The third position, that individuals are indifferent to the income levels and tastes of their neighbors, is also a possibility. We have, then, two reasonable hypotheses about how income levels affect residential choice, and these may be combined with two possible locations, the central city and the suburbs, of firms which accept disadvantaged central-city residents as trainees. We can thus analyze each of the four possible cases for the effects of these training programs on residential location.

Assuming that most of the trainees are nonwhites, any analysis must consider the possible effects of pure discrimination in the housing market. If, for example, firms in the suburbs successfully train and employ central-city nonwhite residents, the existence of racial discrimination in the housing market will prevent these nonwhites from moving to the suburbs. To the extent that this effect exists it will moderate the strength of our results, but it has no effect on the directions of population flow indicated by our discussion.

Consider Case I, in which the Tiebout hypothesis holds and ghetto residents are being trained for jobs in the suburbs. The importance of this case is underlined by the substantial consideration given by manpower planners to problems of transporting ghetto residents to job locations in the suburbs. (See the discussion above.) The Tiebout hypothesis implies that newly trained ghetto residents whose incomes have risen will desire to move to the suburbs in order to live near people with similar income levels and presumably similar desires for certain mixes of publicly produced goods. Furthermore, we would also expect these people to move to the suburbs in order to live closer to their jobs. On both grounds, therefore, this case will result in a migration of more affluent ghetto workers to the suburbs with the resulting further deterioration of the fiscal position of the central cities.

In Case II, in which the Tiebout hypothesis is valid but workers are trained for jobs in the central cities, the results are unclear. On the one hand, their tastes for more affluent neighbors would spur them to move out of the central cities and to the suburbs. On the other hand, their desire to live near their jobs in the central city would help to retain them there. The actual result depends upon the relative strength of each of these two effects.

In the less likely case, in which the Tiebout hypothesis is not valid and where individuals are indifferent about their residential location, the results are determined solely by the location where training occurs. In Case III, in which training is for jobs in the central city, the preferences of workers to reside near their jobs in order to minimize transportation costs will unequivocally lead to an improvement of the position of the central cities. Trained workers who would be receiving higher incomes will desire to live near their jobs and will contribute to the fiscal stability of the central cities in which those jobs are located. If, on the other hand, Case IV holds, where training takes place in the suburbs, we should then expect workers to minimize transportation costs by living near their suburban jobs. In that case, if we assume no offsetting flows of population the fiscal position of the cities will deteriorate as the ghetto residents with higher incomes leave the city.

To the extent that the Tiebout hypothesis is valid and also that most training occurs for jobs in the suburbs, manpower training programs will, over a period of time, exacerbate central-city problems by producing increased emigration of more affluent, successful ghetto trainees to the more wealthy suburbs. If this happens, the remaining population in the cities will consist to an even greater extent than it does now of members of society with the lowest incomes. There is a need for policy measures which link training programs to residential location in order to induce successful trainees to remain in the central cities.

Conclusions About the Relationships Between
Manpower Training and Other Urban
Problems

We have tried to demonstrate in this chapter that substantial interactions may exist between manpower training programs and other facets of urban life. The actual effects of training programs on the potential success of other urban policies depends on a number of parameters as well as on political decisions which society must make. These latter (for example, a decision about which particular sections in an urban area are to be helped by improved transportation) must be made by political leaders. Economists can, however, construct training programs whose positive effects do not produce negative externalities in affecting other urban programs. The structuring of manpower training in urban areas so that it is neutral with respect to other programs should be a minimum requirement of these programs.

6

A Redirection of Manpower Goals, Policy, and Research

In the previous four chapters, we have presented a number of studies designed to illuminate certain aspects of the operation of manpower training programs. Though these were not exhaustive studies of the particular goals around which they centered, they did present some problems and considerations to be used in planning programs aimed at achieving these goals. In this chapter, we use the insights we have developed to discuss possible conflicts among the alternative goals and to present an ideal goal. Finally, we present policy proposals and research programs which might be important in implementing this goal.

Conflicts and Agreements Among the Goals
Under Existing Programs

Helping depressed areas and using manpower programs to help disadvantaged workers are complementary aspects of a similar philosophy. Training programs in both cases are aimed at improving the conditions faced by particular groups of workers—in one case, workers isolated in certain regions of a nation, and in the other, workers distinguished by past economic discrimination against them. In each of these cases, the philosophy is that of direct help by the central government to improve conditions faced by a particular group.

Both workers located in depressed areas and disadvantaged workers isolated in urban ghettoes face labor-market conditions in which there is a substantial excess supply of labor. This similarity is made clear by a comparison of unemployment in depressed areas and unemployment in urban poverty neighborhoods.[1] In both situations it is evident that there is insufficient demand for the skills of the residents of these areas and that adjustments to remove this disequilibrium proceed very slowly.

Conditions under which programs other than manpower training would be more efficient than training programs are similar in both depressed areas and in urban ghettoes. Capital subsidies are especially desirable in both situations if the markets for the products of firms being subsidized are located fairly close to the potential location of the plant. This stipulation implies that

117

capital subsidies should be used in depressed areas located fairly near to the major consumer markets of a nation, and that firms receiving capital subsidies to locate in urban ghettoes be those for which the transport of their final output through congested cities is not too expensive.

Although the goals of helping depressed areas and disadvantaged workers can be pursued as complements, each may conflict quite seriously with attempts to remove bottlenecks in the labor market. The data in Tables 4–6 and 4–7 showed that most shortages of labor are in high-skilled jobs. Assuming that there is no excess demand for unskilled labor, efficient removal of the bottlenecks implied by these shortages of high-skilled labor can be done only by upgrading existing low-skilled employees, not by training the unemployed for high-skilled jobs. Is is clear that the latter training strategy would be less efficient in removing bottlenecks in that it would cost more per worker to train for the high-skilled job.

This discussion suggests that given a fixed training budget we cannot efficiently remove bottlenecks in the labor market and simultaneously help disadvantaged workers directly. If we forego training these workers for the high-skilled jobs in which there are shortages and train them instead for low-skilled jobs, we shall not succeed in removing most of the bottlenecks. A fundamental policy dilemma thus exists: Do we aim manpower training toward directly helping disadvantaged workers, or should it be aimed instead toward removing labor-market shortages as they arise? A similar question can be asked with respect to training in depressed areas and the removal of labor-market shortages. Depressed regions are surely not those in which general shortages of labor exist, so that the allocation of funds to such areas necessarily implies that resources are diverted from the removal of excess demand in the labor market. Here too society must choose between directly helping a particular part of society and improving the economy as a whole.

Disadvantaged nonwhite workers are located disproportionately in the central cities of urban areas, and the main thrust of manpower training has been aimed toward this group.[2] (See the next section for a detailed discussion of this point.) Despite their concentration in cities, manpower training which has as its goal the direct aid of these workers may conflict with the use of manpower training to improve life in urban areas. If manpower programs are used to train disadvantaged workers for low-skilled jobs now held by other workers, the lack of excess demand for such skills implies that the disadvantaged groups will simply displace those workers who have been slightly more fortunate than they. As we discussed in Chapter 2, this displacement effect may increase discontent among nonsubsidized workers and, if this frustration spills over into areas outside the labor market, may heighten tastes for discrimination on the part of the displaced groups. The potential detrimental effects of such an increase in racial friction on life in urban areas are clear.

Efficient use of manpower training as an aid in improving the economy of urban areas may well entail direct help for individuals and groups who cannot be classified as disadvantaged. Subsidies may have to be used to encourage employment of middle-class workers in jobs in the central city in order to prevent the exodus of firms to the suburbs. While such a subsidy might have positive indirect effects on the employment of disadvantaged groups, its main benefit would be for middle-class families.

Training and transportation are linked through their effects on labor-force participation. Maintaining the location of jobs and the residences of middle-class workers in the central city may require improving transportation from central business districts to the neighborhoods in which these workers are domiciled. Given fixed public budgets, improvements in the quality of transportation for the middle class may initially have to be financed at the indirect expense of decreased funds for the training of disadvantaged workers. Although improved transportation may in the long run produce more jobs for lower-income residents, its initial direct effect would be to decrease job opportunities for these workers.

There is no economic conflict between allocating training funds to depressed areas and using training to improve life in urban areas. There is, however, a direct political conflict between achieving these two goals. The depressed areas as designated by the Department of Labor are mainly smaller cities and rural areas (see Table 3–1), while urban policy is generally aimed at the largest metropolitan areas. These differences are likely to lead to legislative conflict between representatives inclined more toward rural interests and those whose constituencies are oriented to urban life. While the removal of bottlenecks in the labor market conflicts with helping depressed areas and disadvantaged workers, there is no necessary conflict between this goal and that of improving the economy of urban areas. Although manpower training is not being used in such a fashion today, it could be structured to provide the impetus for improvement of both the transportation facilities and the fiscal position of the central cities.

Present and Ideal Goals for Manpower Training Programs

There can be little doubt that the prime goal of current manpower training programs in the United States is that of providing direct aid to disadvantaged workers. Numerical evidence showing the great and increasing importance of the young, the uneducated, and the nonwhite in federally sponsored manpower training was presented in Tables 2–1 and 2–2. In addition to this direct evidence, there is the statement of the administrator of federal manpower programs during the years 1965–1969. In this position he "was responsible for attacking the gap relating to employment between the disadvantaged and the manpower institutions of government which are supposed to assist them."[3]

The increasing emphasis on upgrading in federal training programs does not imply that manpower training planners have shifted their focus away from aiding disadvantaged members of the labor force. The official view of the Manpower Administration is that "upgrading is a means of aiding the disadvantaged, and of assuring equal employment opportunities for all races."[4] Although the strategy of upgrading low-level employees rather than training them for entry-level jobs may have some effects in alleviating labor-market shortages, the thrust for upgrading does not stem from this latter source. Rather, it arises from the response of manpower officials to the dissatisfactions expressed by disadvantaged workers who have found themselves trained for low-level, "dead-end" jobs.

Even the provision of the initial version of the proposed Manpower Act of 1969 for an automatic increase in manpower training at high levels of unemployment did not reflect any commitment to a general labor-market policy. Instead, it was based on the belief that, "a timely increase in available manpower program resources can both ease the impact of unemployment for the affected individuals and reduce the pressures which tend to generate further increases in unemployment."[5] The proposals would have used general revenues to train persons who are laid off as the result of deflationary macro-economic policies. Manpower training is seen not as a way of shifting the short-run Phillips curve but rather as a mechanism for transferring the burden of the increased unemployment which results from a move along a Phillips curve.

Despite the fairly strong evidence that manpower training in the United States has as its chief goal helping disadvantaged workers, academic economists maintain the belief that it can also be used to remove shortages in the labor market. One observer defines manpower policies " as programs designed to improve the matching of skills demanded and supplied in the labor market."[6] However, if most of the data on federal manpower training are reasonably accurate, the main effect of training programs has been to match the unemployed with low-level jobs that are already filled by nonsubsidized, low-income workers. Most economists see manpower training as a way of improving the short-run trade-off between unemployment and inflation, but there is no evidence that existing manpower policy has been used to achieve this goal.

Even if we assume that aiding disadvantaged members of the labor force should be the explicit goal of manpower training programs, it is by no means clear that existing programs are most efficient in achieving this goal. We have already noted the potential feedback effect on manpower training appropriations which might arise if disadvantaged workers displace other employees from their accustomed jobs. The strategy of training for entry-level employment suggests that the displacement effect may well be quite substantial. If so, manpower training appropriations could possibly be increased by shifting the emphasis of the programs away from direct aid to the disadvantaged and focusing instead on indirect assistance in the labor market. The latter approach, while it might not produce as much benefit for the disadvantaged workers on a per dollar basis, could result in much larger appropriations for the purposes of training and a greater total amount of help for disadvantaged individuals.

Government subsidies may lock disadvantaged workers into low-level jobs. A worker entering a plant under the aegis of a program which is known to single out disadvantaged workers is hardly likely to be able to mesh into the normal channels of promotion in the plant. (See Chapter 2 for a discussion of this problem.) Recognition of this lock-in effect of past training programs is indicated by the shift in emphasis toward upgrading entry-level workers. While this change in the direction of training programs might improve the lot of the working poor in the short run, it is not certain that the long-run effect is beneficial for them. Unless the jobs into which these workers are being upgraded are those for which shortages exist, training programs will again face the displacement problem and the feedback effect it may produce. Like its predecessors, the upgrading strategy must be tailored to provide subsidies only in those cases where actual shortages exist. Only in this way can it avoid creating competition for jobs between disadvantaged workers and incumbents of higher-level jobs.

Most Northern European countries use manpower training to help achieve low levels of unemployment without rapid rates of inflation. Improving the short-run trade-off between inflation and unemployment should also be the central goal for manpower training in the United States. Although there is some recognition of this goal in the Job Bank program, which disseminates information about existing job vacancies, in no way has it entered the formulation of programs explicitly designed to train workers.[7]

Manpower training is only one of a number of alternative policies that can be used to improve the short-run trade-off between inflation and unemployment. Unfortunately, one of the other policies, the wage-price guidelines of the 1960s, appears to have had at most only a slight effect on the trade-off, and removing racial discrimination in the labor market has proved to be very difficult.[8] Manpower training, on the other hand, has not been used for this purpose, and it could be the most effective tool we have for effecting this structural change in the economy. It could enable the economy to avoid the redistribution of income inherent both in the high inflation produced by past attempts to maintain full employment and the high level of unemployment produced by attempts to reduce inflation to an acceptable level.

Instituting the removal of labor-market shortages as the goal of federally sponsored manpower training could well provide more help to disadvantaged workers than do existing training programs. The major burden of high un-employment rates falls on disadvantaged workers. Improving the trade-off between inflation and unemployment should allow economic policy makers to achieve a lower level of unemployment than has been arrived at in the past. The higher level of aggregate demand and the greater stability of employment generated by that demand should prevent the layoffs of disadvantaged workers which have caused much frustration in the past. Seeing that their careers need not be characterized by numerous intermittent periods of unem-ployment, disadvantaged workers will be more likely to undertake investment in training themselves early in their lives.

Shifting the focus of training programs away from disadvantaged workers and toward labor-market policy also has the beneficial indirect effect of removing the stigma attached to participants in training programs. A labor-market policy should not produce the resentment on the part of existing employed persons which is produced by direct aid to disadvantaged workers. Finally, this indirect creation of jobs for disadvantaged workers through a labor-market policy should prevent these individuals from being locked into low-level jobs and enable them to seek higher-level jobs as vacancies occur.

Policy Proposals to Implement the Goal of Changing the Short-Run Inflation– Unemployment Relationship

In order to achieve efficient use of manpower training funds to remove bottlenecks in the labor market the amount of money available for training should be *increased* when the unemployment rate is low. This "anti-trigger" proposal is the exact opposite of the current strategy of using manpower policy to provide direct help to the disadvantaged and unemployed.[9] Spe-cifically, our anti-trigger proposals would go into effect when the unemploy-ment rate is less than 4 percent and has not risen from its minimum value for more than three consecutive months. This latter requirement is designed to ensure that the government does not begin to inject additional training funds at a time when the economy is receding from a cyclical peak and firms are ceasing their hiring of new workers.

A possible addition to this proposal would be an automatic cutback when the unemployment rate rises above a certain level. Because of the lags in the legislative process it would be desirable to make both this cutback and the automatic trigger as large as possible. In that way, manpower training could be timed flexibly enough to ensure the application of the maximum amount of training funds at those times when the labor market is tightest.

Since 1948, this proposal would have increased funds for training mainly during the Korean War period and from April 1966 through December 1969. Unlike the trigger proposal it would not have increased funds during the period of high unemployment which existed from 1958 to 1961. Training programs are not instantaneous, and there is some possibility that trainees helped under this anti-trigger proposal might enter the labor market when business conditions begin to deteriorate. An examination of unemployment rates from 1948–1969 shows that the average rate facing trainees on completion of their training under the anti-trigger proposal would have been 4.1 percent.[10] This figure compares to 5.4 percent implied by the initial proposals of 1969, and the difference is significant at the 0.1 percent level. Although training takes time, job opportunities facing trainees under the anti-trigger proposal would be much greater than under the trigger idea if the experience of the last twenty-two years is any guide.

Another important consideration in deciding between the trigger and anti-trigger proposals is the durability of skills learned in the training programs. If these skills are fairly durable, it is rational for the government to subsidize more training when unemployment is high and the opportunity cost of the trainees' time is low. As the skills become more perishable, it is increasingly important that trainees find employment quickly, and the anti-trigger increases in desirability. There is no information available on the durability of training in general and on the training subsidized by the government in particular. To the extent, however, that federal training programs encourage the belief that the skills learned will enable the trainees to find employment, the frustration produced when trainees leave the program and cannot find jobs would seem to outweigh the importance of the resource costs involved in training at low rates of unemployment.

As we discussed in Chapter 2, the existing method of sudsidizing on-the-job training and the JOBS program may lead to substantial windfall gains in training for shortage occupations for many participating firms. These windfalls are the result of reimbursement schemes tailored to the nature of the job for which training is being given rather than to the qualifications of the individual being trained. They are a complete waste of government manpower training funds, for they produce no incentive for the firm to increase its own training. Within the framework of the goal of removing bottlenecks from the labor market, the present method of reimbursement can be restructured to ensure that these windfalls do not arise and that firms have as much incentive to undertake training of disadvantaged workers as they do to "cream off" the most qualified members of the labor force entitled to this subsidy.

A better reimbursement method, whether we wish to help disadvantaged workers or the entire labor market, would entail the use of sliding scales depending upon the qualifications of the workers being trained for the specific job. This scale would base subsidies on both the nature of the job being trained for *and* the economic and demographic characteristics of the groups trained under the subsidy program. Points convertible into subsidies would be given based on both of these factors. Firms training younger, less educated workers, as well as those older workers whose skills have become obsolete would qualify for larger subsidies than similar firms training better qualified workers for identical jobs.

The actual amount by which subsidies would differ in relation to the workers' characteristics would have to be determined by a trial-and-error iterative method. An initial subsidy scheme could be set up based upon differential training costs for workers with different backgrounds. If manpower planners find certain groups are being preferred for training over others, the reimbursements for the former group could be cut relative to those of the latter group to induce employers to shift the composition of their trainees. This method of determining the actual subsidies has the advantage of allowing the manpower planner to be guided by the market rather than by an arbitrary system of predetermined subsidies.[11]

The insistence of the original Manpower Development and Training Act of 1962 that occupations for which subsidies are granted be those in which shortages exist is difficult to satisfy with the inadequate information now available on job shortages in local areas. This lack of satisfactory information may have the effect of increasing the possibility that training funds are producing substantial displacement of already employed workers. In order to remedy this, the State Training and Employment Services should provide even more frequent and more detailed information than they now do on occupations in which shortages exist in their jurisdictions. The Manpower Act should be amended to require the explicit use of these job-vacancy surveys in issuing contracts under federal manpower programs. Frequent reporting on local labor-market conditions would ensure that policy could remain flexible enough to meet shortages as they arise. This flexibility will increase the effectiveness of manpower training in achieving an improved trade-off between inflation and unemployment.

The general thrust of manpower training programs should be shifted away from training for low-skilled jobs and toward upgrading workers for high-skilled and technical jobs. This should be a general guideline and is not to be confused with the flexible alternation between granting and removing subsidies for training in different occupations as they shift from shortage to surplus in individual labor markets. The purpose of this rule is to ensure that manpower training is offered only for those jobs in which shortages are likely to exist. In this way, training can proceed with the assurance that it is not merely substituting one unemployed worker for another who is nearly as unfortunate.

Certain occupations should, under this general condition, never qualify for federal subsidies. Entry-level jobs in the service industries and low-level office work certainly fall into this category.[12] These are occupations for which the skills required to learn the specific jobs are so minute as to ensure a sufficient supply of labor even in times of very low aggregate unemployment. By refraining from subsidizing these jobs the government will avoid the use of training funds to produce an effect which the private sector would have produced without the subsidy. On the other hand, there are a number of occupations for which the prior training requirements are large enough to make the supply of labor inadequate except in times of very high unemployment.

Administrative difficulties entailed by a shift to increased upgrading should be no greater than those now encountered by entry-level programs. Contracts could be written to allow firms subsidies for training current employees for jobs on the local list of officially designated shortage occupations. While there are the usual difficulties of determining the appropriate amount of subsidy, research on training costs and the use of the iterative points reimbursement scheme should eventually lead to those subsidies which are correct for each particular move up a job ladder in different industries. Another approach would be to move to a system of grants for some part of training expenditures for upgrading to shortage occupations. As in Great Britain under the Industrial Training Act of 1964, the grants could be based on accounting data showing expenditures *and* on spot-check audits of the quality of training given.[13] In addition to its incentive for upgrading, this approach would have the beneficial effects of both increasing employers' awareness of the amount of training they offer and ensuring that they do not allow their training procedures to deteriorate in quality.

Compared to the combined total of funding of OJT and JOBS training, the amount allocated to institutional training has undergone a relative decline since 1966. This change in the emphasis of federal training programs is the result of congressional disenchantment with the efficacy of institutional training.[14] Since most available studies indicate that on-the-job training is in general more efficient than institutional training, the trend toward the elimination of institutional training should be accelerated, and institutional training might even be abolished entirely. Funds which are now allocated to that program could be shifted toward-on-the-job training. The useful counseling and guidance aspects of institutional programs could be incorporated into federal contracts for on-the-job training.

Manpower subsidies can be used creatively to ameliorate conditions in the nation's cities. Two complementary vital problems facing central cities are the loss of jobs located there and the exodus of middle-class residents to suburban areas. To resolve these problems the government could subsidize the employment of any worker living in the central city who is added to a payroll in a job in the central city in an officially designated shortage occupation. The government might do this by linking its reimbursement to the firm's contribution for the worker to Old Age Survivors Disability and Health Insurance (OASDHI). The actual amount of reimbursement should be high enough to ensure that employers can perceive the value of participating under the subsidy scheme.

This idea would increase middle-class employment and residence in the central city by making city dwellers more attractive to employers for such positions. Indirectly it would induce firms to change their locational decisions in favor of the central city. This indirect effect would have the additional virtue of creating other, nonsubsidized jobs for city residents and would thus tend to ameliorate unemployment in our cities. Because it applies only to workers added to the payroll, it would not provide a windfall for those employers whose existing workers already live in the city.

Tying this proposal to OASDHI has the virtue of administrative simplicity. Each firm already keeps records of its contributions, and it would be a simple matter to use these and the employees' addresses to define eligibility under the subsidy. This ease of administration should overcome employers' unwillingness to participate in the program because of bureaucratic "red tape."

This specific suggestion is only one example of the way in which manpower policy can be combined with urban policy. A complementary scheme designed to subsidize the employment of less-skilled workers in plants in suburban areas might also be introduced. This latter proposal might have the additional desirable effect of increasing employment of low-skilled, nonwhite workers in the suburbs and encouraging them to move near their jobs. This could increase the proportion of nonwhites residing in the suburbs and thus reduce housing segregation in urban areas. Within the framework of subsidizing employment only in shortage occupations, federal subsidy programs can be flexible enough to have beneficial effects on areas not explicitly related to manpower training.

Useful Research for Efficient
Implementation of the Goal

Several important research projects that can be undertaken to help policy makers avoid costly mistakes have been indicated in the course of the discussion in this and the previous chapters. Perhaps the most important is the need to derive better information on the costs of training for different occupations and the amounts by which these costs vary depending upon the skills already embodied in the trainees. This information could be extremely useful in instituting the points-system reimbursement scheme outlined in the previous section. It would enable the government to fix an initial set of subsidies which would not be very far removed from the final equilibrium set. As a complement to the project on training costs it is necessary to derive estimates of the generality and specificity of training by occupation. We demonstrated in Chapter 3 how important this distinction would be for manpower policy in a depressed area; it would also be useful knowledge in the structuring of subsidies for on-the-job training.

It is admittedly very difficult to derive data on training costs for individual jobs. The only approach which has any promise is a microeconomic set of studies using costing analysis. There is a long tradition of this type of study at the plant level, and there is no reason why it could not be extended to itemize training as a separate component of costs.[15]

Although our major goal is that of removing bottlenecks from the labor market, a limited training budget implies that we need to choose from among the shortage occupations those which are to be subsidized. Our method would be to pick those occupations which generate the greatest amount of job creation at the lower levels of skill. In that manner we can simultaneously achieve our general labor-market goal while producing the greatest impact among disadvantaged workers. To do this, we need to know the elasticities of substitution among various high-level and low-level occupations.

There has been some work on the aggregate level on the estimation of substitution elasticities among different skills, and this information suggests that the elasticities are in general quite high.[16] For the purpose of manpower policy, we need more detailed information about the extent to which different occupations are substitutes or complements. Further disaggregation by occupational class and the econometric estimation of the parameters of the disaggregated production functions are necessary.

In order to use manpower policy to alleviate shortages in the labor market we need to know which occupations could be classified in that category. We need to be able to distinguish between those occupations in which employers are exercising their monopsony power and refusing to pay a wage sufficient to call forth trained labor, and those other occupations in which trained labor would not be forthcoming in the short run in sufficient quantities at any price. This information is essential both so that the government does not subsidize occupations in which shortages do not exist, and also so that we do not provide subsidies to aid employers in the use of their exploitative labor-market power.

There has been a large increase in the extent of data available on job vacancies in individual labor markets. Even now, however, only a small fraction of what must be classified as vacancies are listed with the State Training and Employment Service and are thus available for use in the planning of manpower policy. It is essential that this percentage be increased, either through research by state agencies or through some method which induces firms to list more of their vacancies. One method might be to offer a small subsidy to firms for each vacancy listed with the state. While this proposal would have the possibly detrimental effect of increasing turnover, this drawback might be offset by the value of improvements in manpower policy made possible by the better job-vacancy data that would be produced.

The Need for a Redirection of Manpower Activities

With only a few exceptions, the work by economists on questions of manpower training policy has been prompted by the desire to evaluate specific federal and local manpower programs. While such evaluation is important, there is a clear lack of basic research in this area. More effort should be expended to answer questions such as those raised in the previous section as well as other basic questions necessary for an efficient pursuit of a rational labor-market policy.

The best assurance of full employment is an efficient labor market in which the government is an active participant in providing training for workers in order to meet shortages in specific occupations. Despite the great desire to give direct help to the poor and the unemployed, direct aid may very well be an inefficient way of producing this desired goal. If, instead, manpower training is used to enable the economy to maintain low unemployment with only moderate rates of inflation, the unemployed and the disadvantaged can be absorbed in jobs in the private sector efficiently and without any special help.

Notes

Chapter 1

1. The enabling legislation which created the Works Progress Administration was passed in order "to increase employment by providing for useful projects." (74th Congress, 1st Session, Public Resolution 11.)

2. U.S. Code 75 Stat. 47.

3. U.S. Code 76 Stat. 24.

4. U.S. Code 78 Stat. 508. This act entailed the initial programs of the so-called War on Poverty.

5. This estimate is based on the figure for 1958 provided by Jacob Mincer, "On-the-Job Training: Costs, Returns, and Implications," *Journal of Political Economy* 70, Pt. 2 (October 1962): 57. The estimate for 1958 was prorated using the gross national product in current dollars for both 1958 and 1969.

6. Computed using estimates of time spent in on-the-job investment after the completion of formal schooling multiplied by the average wage during the investment period. The estimates were calculated for four race–sex groups and aggregated according to each group's importance in the civilian labor force using data in Bureau of Labor Statistics, *Bulletin 1666*, p. 46. The foregone earnings estimates are calculated from Ronald Oaxaca, "Male–Female Wage Differentials in Urban Labor Markets," Ph.D. dissertation, Princeton University, 1971.

7. Some of these histories of the legislative and administrative aspects of manpower programs are excellent pieces of analysis and research. See, for example, Sar Levitan and Garth Mangum, *Federal Training and Work Programs in the Sixties* (Ann Arbor, Michigan: Institute of Labor and Industrial Relations, 1969); also Garth Mangum, *The Emergence of Manpower Policy* (New York: Holt, Rinehart and Winston, 1969).

8. Two examples of this genre are David Page, "Retraining Under the Manpower Development Act," *Public Policy* 13 (1964): 266; and Glen Cain and Ernst Stromsdorfer, "An Economic Evaluation of Government Training Programs in West Virginia," in Gerald Somers, ed., *Retraining the Unemployed* (Madison: University of Wisconsin Press, 1968).

9. An examination of research contracts under the MDTA in effect during fiscal year 1969 showed that 74 out of 92 projects could be classified as specific analyses of data applying either to a local area or to an individual

industry. Most of the remaining 18 projects were general discussions of existing manpower training programs. (Calculated from Manpower Administration, *Manpower Research Projects*, 1969.)

10. A fine example of the value of such interview work is Robert Goldfarb, "The Evaluation of Government Programs," *Yale Economic Essays* 9 (Fall 1969): 58–106.

11. Eli Ginzberg, *Manpower Agenda for America* (New York: McGraw-Hill, 1968), p. 225, presents a discussion of possible manpower goals including such completely general ones as "the full development of human potential." He also lists as specific goals those discussed in this study.

12. Many of the theoretical problems of growth are discussed in Edmund Phelps, *Golden Rules of Economic Growth* (New York: Norton, 1966). The literature in this area burgeoned during the 1960s.

Chapter 2

1. S. 974, 89th Congress, 1st Session, a bill introduced by Senator Joseph Clark in February 1965.

2. Statement of Secretary of Labor W. Willard Wirtz before Senate Subcommittee on Employment and Manpower, 88:1, July 16, 1963, p. 26.

3. Statement of Representative William Avery of Kansas, *Congressional Record*, House of Representatives, 87:2, p. 2999.

4. Statement of Representative H. R. Gross of Iowa, ibid.

5. *New York Times*, December 20, 1969, p. 1.

6. *Ibid.*, February 4, 1969, p. 1.

7. See Milton Friedman, *A Theory of the Consumption Function* (Princeton: Princeton University Press, 1957), p. 70, for evidence that spending propensities out of permanent income differ only slightly across income classes.

8. Glen Cain and Ernst Stromsdorfer, "An Economic Evaluation of Government Training Programs in West Virginia," in Gerald Somers, ed., *Retraining the Unemployed* (Madison: University of Wisconsin Press, 1968), p. 335.

9. David Page, "Retraining Under the Manpower Development Act," *Public Policy* 13 (1964): 266.

10. Michael Borus, "A Benefit-Cost Analysis of the Economic Effectiveness of Retraining the Unemployed," *Yale Economic Essays* 4 (Fall 1964): 397.

11. Sar Levitan and Garth Mangum, *Federal Training and Work Programs in the Sixties* (Ann Arbor, Michigan: Institute of Labor and Industrial Relations, 1969), p. 33.

12. Cain and Stromsdorfer, *op. cit.*, pp. 311–312.

13. Robert Goldfarb, "The Evaluation of Government Programs," *Yale Economic Essays* 9 (Fall 1969): 71–72.

14. See Harold Watts, "Graduated Work Incentives: An Experiment in Negative Taxation," *American Economic Review* 59 (May 1969): 463–472, for a description of this experiment.

15. The basic elements of this program are reported in the *New York Times*, January 21, 1970, p. 27.

16. Specific training includes any expenditure which raises a worker's productivity in the firm making the outlay but which has no effect on his productivity elsewhere. See Gary Becker, *Human Capital* (New York: National Bureau of Economic Research, 1964), pp. 18–19.

17. Several studies have been unable to reject the hypothesis that the elasticity of substitution equals one. See Charles Bischoff, "Hypothesis Testing and the Demand for Capital Goods," *Review of Economics and Statistics* 51 (August 1969): 354–368; and Paul Zarembka, "On the Empirical Relevance of the CES Production Function," *Review of Economics and Statistics* 52 (February 1970): 47–53.

18. Finis Welch, "Education in Production," *Journal of Political Economy* 78 (January 1970): 51.

19. John Burton and John Parker, "Interindustry Variations in Voluntary Labor Mobility," *Industrial and Labor Relations Review* 22 (January 1969): 199–216, present a regression model in which industries with higher levels of earnings are shown to have lower turnover rates. John Pencavel, *An Analysis of the Quit Rate in American Manufacturing Industry* (Princeton, N.J.: Industrial Relations Section, 1970), p. 21, corroborates this result in a somewhat more sophisticated model.

20. See, for example, the discussion of the difficulties facing suburban firms in metropolitan New York, *New York Times*, April 13, 1970, p. 82.

21. For example, Morton Baratz, et al., *The Baltimore CAP Evaluation Study* (University of Pennsylvania, Institute for Environmental Studies, June 1970), (mimeo.), p. 533, present evidence to this effect in the case of a journey-to-work subsidy offered to disadvantaged workers.

22. This problem has been cited in numerous case studies of training programs. (Cf. Cain and Stromsdorfer, *op. cit.*, p. 310.)

23. Jacob Mincer, "On-the-Job Training: Costs, Returns and Implications," *Journal of Political Economy* 70, Pt. 2 (October 1962): 68, presents evidence that the amount of on-the-job training is positively related to the level of formal schooling. Lester Thurow, *Poverty and Discrimination* (Wash-

ington, D.C.: Brookings Institution, 1969), pp. 70–72, discusses the complementarities between OJT and formal education.

24. Statement in "An Open Door for American Labor," radio address of October 21, 1968, reprinted in Bureau of National Affairs, *Daily Labor Report*, October 22, 1968, p. E–1.

25. Louis Harris and Associates, *Sources of Racial and Religious Tensions in New York City* (New York: Louis Harris and Associates, 1969), p. 332.

26. *Ibid.*, p. 135.

27. Lois Wille, "Fear Rises in the Suburbs," one of a series of articles in *Chicago Daily News*, February 25, 1970, based on interviews in Chicago's ethnic neighborhoods; and *New York Times*, August 17, 1970, p. 18. The memorandum to the Secretary of Labor by Assistant Secretary Jerome Rosow, *The Problem of the Blue-Collar Worker*, is dated April 16, 1970, and was released August 13, 1970.

28. Bureau of National Affairs, *Daily Labor Report*, September 5, 1968, pp. A–8, A–9.

29. One of the many discussions of this problem by business groups is National Industrial Conference Board, *Education, Training, and Employment of the Disadvantaged* (New York: National Industrial Conference Board, 1969), pp. 9–10.

Chapter 3

1. Our ignoring migration subsidies in no way implies that they are an unimportant means of helping depressed areas. Indeed, Niles Hansen, *Rural Poverty and the Urban Crisis* (Bloomington, Indiana: University of Indiana Press, 1970), argues persuasively that the problems of many such areas could be alleviated by subsidies to move their inhabitants to medium-sized cities. He does not, however, discuss how the political problems associated with this policy might be overcome. The magnitude of the problems is suggested by George Borts and Jerome Stein, *Economic Growth in a Free Market* (New York: Columbia University Press, 1964), pp. 197–198.

2. U.S. President, *Economic Report of the President*, 1955, p. 61.

3. U.S. Code 75 Stat. 47.

4. The idea for the premium is presented in the Green Paper, *The Development Areas: A Proposal for a Regional Employment Premium*, H.M. Treasury, Department of Economic Affairs, HMSO, April 5, 1967.

5. Economic Council of Canada, *Economic Goals for Canada for 1970* (Ottawa: Queen's Printer, 1964), p. 201.

6. Gary Becker, *Human Capital* (New York: National Bureau of Economic Research, 1964), pp. 18–31.

7. The solution to this pair of equations maximizes the firm's profits, for:

$$\frac{\partial^2 \pi}{\partial m^2} = -ES^*q''(m) < 0$$

$$\frac{\partial^2 \pi}{\partial E^2} = pf''(E) < 0$$

and

$$\frac{\partial^2 \pi}{\partial m \, \partial E} = 0$$

8. The evidence on this last point is fairly clear. Lloyd Reynolds, *The Structure of Labor Markets* (New York: Harper, 1951), p. 215, and other labor market studies find that less than half of the workers who quit have jobs which they have already secured.

9. See Daniel Hamermesh, "Spectral Analysis of the Relationship between Gross Changes in Employment and Changes in Output," *Review of Economics and Statistics* 51 (February 1969): 62–69, for some evidence on this point.

10. See Borts and Stein, *op. cit.*, p. 198, for a discussion of this.

11. Economic Council of Canada, *The Challenge of Growth and Change* (Ottawa: Queen's Printer, 1968), p. 167. The actual amount of investment produced by this subsidy was $1.8 billion, so that government participation in investment in these areas amounted to approximately one-fifth of the total investment.

12. Area Redevelopment Administration, *Economic Growth in American Communities* (Washington, D.C.: U.S. Government Printing Office, 1963), p. 13; and Economic Development Administration, *Jobs for America* (Washington, D.C.: U.S. Government Printing Office, 1969), p. 6. In contrast to the Canadian regional program, area capital subsidies in the United States comprise the bulk of total investment undertaken under the subsidy program.

13. R. G. D. Allen, *Mathematical Analysis for Economists* (London: Macmillan, 1960), p. 343.

14. Phoebus Dhrymes, "Some Extensions and Tests of the CES Class of Production Functions," *Review of Economics and Statistics* 47 (November 1965): 357–366, presents evidence for the existence of this dichotomy between the two types of industry. Zvi Griliches, "More on CES Production Functions," *Review of Economics and Statistics* 49 (November 1967): 608–611,

produces estimates which, while they are not so strong as those of Dhrymes, do still indicate a tendency for this difference to exist.

Chapter 4

1. Milton Friedman, "The Role of Monetary Policy," *American Economic Review* 58 (March 1968): 7–11. Friedman argues that in the long run real wages will be adjusted rather than money wages, so that unemployment cannot deviate from an amount indicated by aggregate supply. Friedman's verbal model has been made rigorous by Robert Lucas and Leonard Rapping, "Price Expectations and the Phillips Curve," *American Economic Review* 59 (June 1969): 342–350.

2. Richard Lipsey, "The Relation Between Unemployment and the Rate of Change of Money Wage Rates in the United Kingdom, 1862–1957," *Economica*, N. S., 27 (February 1960): 1–31.

3. Council of Economic Advisors, *Annual Report*, 1963, p. 84.

4. *New York Times*, May 6, 1969, p. 1.

5. Address by President Richard Nixon, "The Rising Cost of Living," October 17, 1969, as reported in Bureau of National Affairs, *Daily Labor Report*, October 17, 1969, p. X–2.

6. William Peirce, "Selective Manpower Policy and the Trade-Off Between Rising Prices and Unemployment," Ph.D. dissertation, Princeton University, 1966.

7. Charles Holt, "Improving the Labor Market Trade-Off Between Inflation and Unemployment," *American Economic Review* 59 (May 1969): 135–147.

8. The work of Dale Mortenson, "A Theory of Wage and Employment Dynamics," in Edmund Phelps, *Microeconomic Foundations of Employment and Inflation Theory* (New York: Norton, 1970), and "Job Search, the Duration of Unemployment and the Phillips Curve," *American Economic Review* 60 (December 1970): 847–862, provides the theoretical foundation for the job-search view of the Phillips curve.

9. Charles Holt et al., *Planning Production, Inventories and Work Force* (Englewood Cliffs, N.J.: Prentice-Hall, 1960), ch. 2, prove the result that a quadratic adjustment cost function leads the profit-maximizing firm to lag its adjustment of the decision variable. A good exposition of reasons for the quadratic nature of this function can be found in Ronald Soligo, "The Short-Run Relationship Between Employment and Output," *Yale Economic Essays* 6 (Spring 1966): 174.

10. Lipsey, *op. cit.*

11. This notation means that Z is simply the remainder of a division of t by 20. For example, if t is 72, Z is 12.

12. This relative duration of expansions and contractions is slightly less than that used by the National Bureau of Economic Research in its reference cycles. With the exception of the long expansion of the 1960s, the average expansion is nearly three times as long as the average contraction. John Firestone, *Federal Receipts and Expenditures During Business Cycles, 1879–1958* (Princeton, N.J.: Princeton University Press, 1960), p. 4.

13. Daniel Hamermesh, "A Disaggegative Econometric Model of Gross Changes in Employment," *Yale Economic Essays* 9 (Fall 1969): 130.

14. Marc Nerlove, *The Dynamics of Supply* (Baltimore: Johns Hopkins Press, 1958), derives this lag structure and demonstrates the equivalence of the adjustment and expectations theories underlying this formulation of the lag.

15. The estimated rate of deaths and retirements of United States males in all occupations is exactly 2 percent per year of total employment in that category. See Bureau of Labor Statistics, *Bulletin 1606*, p. 64.

16. Sidney and Beatrice Webb, *Industrial Democracy* (London: Longmans Green, 1920), pp. 715–739, argue that union wage policy will lead to wages which are rigid downward. J. M. Keynes, *The General Theory of Employment, Interest, and Money* (New York: Harcourt, Brace and World, 1964), pp. 257–269, implies that downward wage rigidity may be widespread and uses it to differentiate his system from the classical case.

17. In the years 1932–1969, the only ones for which data are available, average hourly earnings in manufacturing declined only between 1932 and 1933. Bureau of Labor Statistics, *Bulletin 1630*, p. 182.

18. The importance of the second variable has been demonstrated fairly conclusively in empirical studies covering the postwar period. Cf. Alfred Tella, "Labor Force Sensitivity to Employment by Age, Sex," *Industrial Relations* 4 (February 1965): 69–83; and Thomas Dernburg and Kenneth Strand, "Hidden Unemployment, 1953–62," *American Economic Review* 56 (March 1966): 71–95.

19. William Bowen and T. Finegan, *The Economics of Labor Force Participation* (Princeton, N.J.: Princeton University Press, 1969), p. 513.

20. Paul Douglas, *The Theory of Wages* (New York: Macmillan, 1934), pp. 205–207. Irving Kravis, "Relative Income Shares in Fact and Theory," *American Economic Review* 49 (December 1959): 917–949, presents a number of alternative estimates of labor's share of output.

21. A lag of approximately this duration was found by Soligo, *op. cit.*; Hamermesh, *op. cit.*; and Ray Fair, *The Short Run Demand for Workers and Hours* (Amsterdam: North-Holland Publishing, 1969). The only study in which a much longer lag was estimated is that of Edwin Kuh, "Income Distribution and Employment Over the Business Cycle," in James Duesenberry et al., *The Brookings Quarterly Econometric Model of the United States* (Chicago: Rand McNally, 1965).

22. Computed from Bureau of Labor Statistics, *Employment and Earnings* (February 1970), p. 56.

23. Based on data in George Perry, *Unemployment, Money Wage Rates and Inflation* (Cambridge, Mass.: The M.I.T. Press, 1966), pp. 129–131.

24. The most prominent use of this form of the unemployment rate is Perry, *ibid.*, p. 39. The inverse of the unemployment rate has also been used by N. J. Simler and Alfred Tella, "Labor Reserves and the Phillips Curve," *Review of Economics and Statistics* 50 (February 1968): 32–49.

25. In the trucking industry's Transportation Opportunity Program this important indirect effect has been especially pronounced. See Bureau of National Affairs, *Manpower Information Service* (August 12, 1970), pp. 18–19.

26. John Dunlop, "The Task of Contemporary Wage Theory," in George Taylor and Frank Pierson, eds., *New Concepts in Wage Determination* (New York: McGraw-Hill, 1957), pp. 128–139, discusses job clusters in a plant and the job ladders within them.

27. *Manpower Report of the President*, 1970, p. 304.

28. Charles Metcalf, "The Size Distribution of Personal Income in an Econometric Model of the United States," Ph.D. dissertation, Massachusetts Institute of Technology, 1968; and Robinson Hollister and John Palmer, "The Impact of Inflation on the Poor," University of Wisconsin, Institute for Research on Poverty, 1969 (mimeo.).

Chapter 5

1. Gerald Breese, *Urbanization in Newly Developing Countries* (Englewood Cliffs, N.J.: Prentice-Hall, 1966), pp. 12–37, presents detailed data on the growth and extent of urbanization during the last century in most nations of the world.

2. Stanley Ruttenberg, *Manpower Challenge of the 1970s* (Baltimore: Johns Hopkins Press, 1970), p. 2. The statements of Senator Joseph Clark during the hearings on the proposed MDTA amendments in 1968 also indicate

that an important motivation for these changes stemmed from the disturbances which took place in the cities during the previous year. (Senate Subcommittee on Employment, Manpower and Poverty, *Hearings*, March 13, 1968).

3. See Bureau of National Affairs, *Manpower Information Service* (July 1, 1970), p. 5, for a detailed discussion of the role of the mayors in federal manpower programs. During May 1970, the JOBS program allocated 94 percent of its funds to training within metropolitan areas. (*Ibid.*, Reference File, July 1970).

4. Preamble to S. 3063, 90th Congress, 2nd Session, a bill introduced by Senator Joseph Clark in February 1968.

5. Oscar Ornati, *Transportation Needs of the Poor* (New York: Praeger, 1969); and James Sundquist, "Jobs, Training and Welfare for the Underclass," in Kermit Gordon, ed., *Agenda for the Nation* (Washington, D.C.: Brookings Institution, 1968), p. 57, discuss this problem and offer possible solutions outside of the existing transportation system.

6. See, for example, Bureau of National Affairs, *Manpower Information Service* (January 14, 1970), p. 25.

7. Computed from Bureau of Census, *Current Population Reports*, P-23, No. 27, (February 1969). Edwin Mills, "Urban Density Functions," *Urban Studies* 7 (February 1970): 5–20, presents a detailed discussion and data illustrating this point.

8. Among the studies discussing labor mobility on an interindustry basis are Sumner Slichter, *The Turnover of Factory Labor* (New York: Appleton, 1921); Lloyd Ulman, "Labor Mobility and the Industrial Wage Structure in the Postwar United States," *Quarterly Journal of Economics* 79 (February 1965): 73–97; Organization for Economic Cooperation and Development, *Wages and Labour Mobility* (Paris: OECD, 1965); John Burton and John Parker, "Inter-Industry Variations in Voluntary Labor Mobility," *Industrial and Labor Relations Review* 22 (January 1969): 199–216; Daniel Hamermesh, "A Disaggregative Econometric Model of Gross Changes in Employment," *Yale Economic Essays* 9 (Fall 1969): 107–145; and John Pencavel, *An Analysis of the Quit Rate in American Manufacturing Industry* (Princeton, N.J.: Industrial Relations Section, 1970). Some of the studies analyzing mobility in urban areas are Lloyd Reynolds, *The Structure of Labor Markets* (New York: Harper, 1951); Gladys Palmer, *Labor Mobility in Six Cities* (New York: Social Science Research Council, 1954); and Herbert Parnes, *Research on Labor Mobility* (New York: Social Science Research Council, 1954).

9. With the exception of Slichter, all of the studies of interindustry mobility cited in the previous footnote have been concerned with this question.

10. Walter Oi, "Labor as a Quasi-Fixed Factor," *Journal of Political Economy* 70 (December 1962): 545, presents a detailed discussion of the way in which investment in specific training affects labor mobility. Pencavel, *op. cit.*, pp. 11–13, discusses in mathematical terms this same calculation.

11. This point is presented in detail in Hamermesh, *op. cit.*, pp. 114–115.

12. Larry Sjaastad, "The Costs and Returns of Human Migration," *Journal of Political Economy* 70, Pt. 2 (October 1962): 84–85, discusses this and other aspects of migration within the framework of human capital theory.

13. Palmer, *op. cit.*, p. 67; OECD, *op. cit.*, p. 56; and Pencavel, *op. cit.*, p. 30, all demonstrate that a worker's voluntary mobility decreases with age.

14. The evidence that women tend to have higher rates of voluntary mobility than men is supported in the studies by OECD, *op. cit.*, p. 60; Burton and Parker, *op. cit.*, p. 210; and Pencavel, *op. cit.*, p. 30.

15. This evidence is presented in Parnes, *op. cit.*, pp. 116–118; and in Burton and Parker, *op. cit.*, p. 210.

16. See Franklin Fisher, "Dynamic Structure and Estimation in Economy-Wide Econometric Models," in James Duesenberry et al., eds., *The Brookings Quarterly Econometric Model of the United States* (Chicago: Rand NcNally, 1965), pp. 589–635.

17. The estimating equation is $q = \alpha + \beta WM + \varepsilon$, where WM is the money wage rate. Assume

$$WM = \gamma WR; \qquad \gamma > 1, \tag{a}$$

The assumption on γ reflects the observation that real wages are positively correlated with the cost of living.

Then $\hat{\beta} = (\text{cov } WM \cdot q)/(\text{var } WM)$, where the superior carat denotes a parameter estimate. Substituting (a) for WM

$$\hat{\beta} = \frac{\gamma \text{ cov } WR \cdot q}{\gamma^2 \text{ var } WR} \tag{b}$$

The true equation is $q = \alpha' + \beta' WR + \varepsilon'$, and

$$\hat{\beta}' = (\text{cov } WR \cdot q)/(\text{var } WR) \tag{c}$$

Comparing (b) and (c), $|\hat{\beta}'| > |\hat{\beta}|$ if $\gamma > 1$.

18. The data on quit rates and average weekly earnings by labor market are from Bureau of Labor Statistics, *Employment and Earnings*, May 1965 and May 1970. Area unemployment rate data are available in U.S. President,

Manpower Report of the President, 1970. The remaining data on migration, nonwhite and female population, and the age distribution of the population are all presented in Bureau of the Census, *Census of Population, 1960*, vol. 1, pt. 1.

19. Stephen Goldfeld and Richard Quandt, "Some Tests for Homoscedasticity," *Journal of the American Statistical Association* 60 (June 1965): 539–547.

20. See Richard Lester, *Manpower Planning in a Free Society* (Princeton, N.J.: Princeton University Press, 1966), p. 141, for a discussion of different definitions of mobility.

21. The system of *nenkō joretsu* gives rise to an extremely low rate of labor mobility. For a discussion of this practice and its effects on wage differentials see Solomon Levine, "Labor Markets and Collective Bargaining in Japan," in William Lockwood, ed., *The State and Economic Enterprise in Japan* (Princeton, N.J.: Princeton University Press, 1965), pp. 633–668.

22. Assume that only the West and the Northeast are in the sample and that we have the same number of observations on each. By definition

$$\hat{\varepsilon}_i = q_i - \hat{\alpha} - \hat{\beta} W M_i \tag{a}$$

$$\hat{\varepsilon}_i' = q_i - \hat{\alpha}' - \hat{\beta}' W R_i \tag{b}$$

Using the same notation as in footnote 17, we postulate that $\gamma_{ne} > \gamma_w > 1$. This assumption is corroborated by comparing budgets for these areas in the continental United States (Bureau of Labor Statistics, *Handbook of Labor Statistics*, 1969, p. 340) especially when Honolulu and Los Angeles are deleted from the calculations. Taking averages in (a) and (b) for observations in the West and those in the Northeast; and substituting for WM in (a) for each region, and observing that $\hat{\alpha} = \hat{\alpha}'$, we have

$$\bar{\hat{\varepsilon}}_w' - \bar{\hat{\varepsilon}}_w = [-\hat{\beta}' + \hat{\beta}\gamma_w]\overline{WR}_w \tag{c}$$

$$\bar{\hat{\varepsilon}}_{ne}' - \hat{\varepsilon}_{ne} = [-\hat{\beta}' + \hat{\beta}\gamma_{ne}]\overline{WR}_{ne} \tag{d}$$

where the superior bar denotes an average over the subscripted region. Now the sum of the left-hand sides of (c) and (d) is zero by the Gauss–Markov theorem, so that

$$[-\hat{\beta}' + \hat{\beta}\gamma_w]\overline{WR}_w + [-\hat{\beta}' + \hat{\beta}\gamma_{ne}]\overline{WR}_{ne} = 0 \tag{e}$$

Since the sum of the terms in (e) is zero, one must be positive and the other negative. But $\gamma_{ne} > \gamma_w$ by hypothesis, so $|\hat{\beta}\gamma_{ne}| > |\hat{\beta}\gamma_w|$, and since both $\hat{\beta}$ and $\hat{\beta}'$ are negative, the first term must be positive and the second negative. Thus $\bar{\varepsilon}'_w > \bar{\varepsilon}_w > 0$ and $\bar{\varepsilon}'_{ne} < \bar{\varepsilon}'_{ne} < 0$, and a regression based on appropriate data would, under our assumption about interregional differences in the cost of living, produce more significant differences in the average residuals.

23. Paul Offner, "Labor Force Participation in the Ghetto," Ph.D. dissertation, Princeton University, 1970.

24. John Kain and John Meyer, "Transportation and Poverty," *Public Interest* 18 (Winter 1970): 81. The materials cited in footnote 5 also provide evidence that these activities are interrelated.

25. See, for example, John Meyer, John Kain, and Martin Wohl, *The Urban Transportation Problem* (Cambridge, Mass.: Harvard University Press, 1965), pp. 83–107.

26. Samuel Bowles, "Aggregation of Labor Inputs in the Economics of Growth and Planning," *Journal of Political Economy* 78 (January 1970): 68–81. The largest value for any elasticity estimated in this study is 5.9.

27. Charles Tiebout, "A Pure Theory of Local Expenditures," *Journal of Political Economy* 64 (October 1956): 416–424.

Chapter 6

1. The unemployment rate in urban poverty neighborhoods averaged 5.5 percent during 1969 compared to a national average of 3.5 percent. *Manpower Report of the President*, 1970, p. 295.

2. In 1970, 78.8 percent of nonwhite families living in urbanized areas lived in the central cities of those areas. This figure contrasts to 41.3 percent for the white population. Bureau of the Census, *Current Population Reports*, P–23, No. 27 (February 1969), p. 39.

3. Stanley Ruttenberg, *Manpower Challenge of 1970s* (Baltimore: Johns Hopkins Press, 1970), p. vii.

4. William Kolberg, "Upgrading the Working Poor," *Manpower* (November 1969), p. 25. A similar view is expressed by Ray Marshall, "Reflections on Upgrading," *Manpower* (January 1970), pp. 3–7, and by Frank Riessman and Hermine Popper, *Up From Poverty* (New York: Harper, 1968), p. 8.

5. Section 501 of S. 2838, 91st Congress, 1st Session, bill introduced by Senator Jacob Javits in August 1969.

6. Lester Thurow, " The Role of Manpower Policy in Achieving Aggregate Goals," in Robert Gordon, ed., *Toward a Manpower Policy* (New York: Wiley, 1967), p. 72. The remarks by William Bowen and Bertil Olsson are also indicative of a preoccupation of academic economists with this role of manpower policy.

7. The Job Bank was also included in the proposed Manpower Training Act of 1969 as Title IV.

8. Although wage changes during the early 1960s were somewhat lower than could have been explained using wage equations based on the 1950s, a number of explanations other than the guideposts have been offered for this result. See, for example, N. J. Simler and Alfred Tella, " Labor Reserves and the Phillips Curve," *Review of Economics and Statistics* 50 (February 1968): 32–49.

9. The Nixon Administration proposal (see footnote 5), which was deleted from the final bill vetoed by the President in December 1970, provided for an automatic 10 percent increase in training funds in any month in which the unemployment rate is greater than 4.5 percent and has been so for three consecutive months.

10. Sar Levitan and Garth Mangum, *Federal Training and Work Programs in the Sixties* (Ann Arbor, Michigan: Institute of Labor and Industrial Relations, 1969), p. 79, present data on the duration of institutional training programs for 1963–1967. The average duration using enrollments as weights is 6.5 months; we use 7 months in our calculation in order to allow for delays in reporting the unemployment data. The average unemployment rates under the two proposals were computed using this duration of training and the unemployment data in Bureau of Labor Statistics, *Employment and Earnings* (February 1970), p. 55.

11. An iterative technique using the market to determine the appropriate subsidy has been proposed by one observer for use in dealing with problems of water pollution: William Baumol, "On Taxation and the Control of Externalities," Princeton University, 1970 (mimeo.).

12. Examples of MDTA contracts for training in occupations which could in no sense by considered in shortage are abundant. In Chicago, in October 1969, the Department of Labor let a contract for $160,000 for institutional training of 100 general clerks. In December 1969, subsidies of $130,000 were offered in Texas for on-the-job training of 100 short-order cooks. Bureau of National Affairs, *Manpower Information Service, Reference File*, 1015/4 and 1035/6a.

13. See Gary Hansen, *Britain's Industrial Training Act* (Washington, D.C.:

National Manpower Policy Task Force, 1967), pp. 42–47, for a discussion of the British systems of grants for training.

14. Garth Mangum, *Contributions and Costs of Manpower Development and Training* (Ann Arbor, Michigan: Institute of Labor and Industrial Relations, 1967), pp. 66–69, presents a detailed summary of a number of cost-benefit studies illustrating this point.

15. An early precursor of cost-accounting studies is Joel Deane, *Statistical Cost Functions of a Hosiery Mill* (Chicago: University of Chicago Press, 1941). Charles Holt et al., *Planning Production, Inventories and Work Force* (Englewood Cliffs, N.J.: Prentice-Hall, 1960), present a detailed cost study in which attention is paid to deriving cost functions for both direct and indirect charges associated with employment.

16. Samuel Bowles, "Aggregation of Labor Inputs in the Economics of Growth and Planning," *Journal of Political Economy* 78 (January 1970): 68–81.

Index

143

About the Author

Daniel S. Hamermesh is an assistant professor of economics at Princeton University. He received his B.A. from the University of Chicago and his Ph.D. from Yale University. His previous work on the relationships between gross changes in employment and wage rates, on the Phillips curve, and on the effects of white-collar unions on wages has appeared in the major scholarly journals in economics in the United States.